Super Scrimpers

Super Scrimpers

LIVE LIFE FOR HALF THE PRICE

CONTENTS

Dear Supercrimper ,

*Britain has a fine tradition of resourcefulness and it's time
we brought back the ingenuity of the past to make better
lives for ourselves today. This book will help you on your way
and give you the tools you need to add some style to your life
without breaking the bank.*

Those of you who watch Superscrimpers *will know that
the members of my Superscrimper army are the experts
at showing us all how to live well for less in these difficult
financial times. Here, at last, their nuggets of wisdom are
collected for your reference.*

*With enough money-saving ideas to banish the financial
blues for good, this book shows us all how to be more clever
with our cash. There are ingenious, penny-pinching tips by
the bucket load, including household tricks your grandmother
used to know, recipes for leftovers and foraged treats, ideas for
customizing old clothes and for upcycling pre-loved furniture
to add a little glamour to your home. Plus you'll find recipes
for beauty products using household ingredients and DIY
and garden fixes that won't cost the earth.*

*Be inspired to save your money and change your life
– get Superscrimping!*

Mrs Moneypenny

IN THE
KITCHEN

THE AVERAGE FAMILY THROWS AWAY £680 OF FOOD EVERY YEAR. THAT'S £12 BILLION OF FOOD GOING TO WASTE ANNUALLY IN THE UK.

Source: Wrap 2010

In the 1940s nothing went to waste and we can learn a lot from our superscrimping forebears. By ditching premium brands, heading to our local markets and cooking from scratch using seasonal ingredients we can serve up plenty of tasty savings. And cheap doesn't have to mean cheerless — herbs, spices and a canny way with leftovers put the gastronomy back into food economy.

We've assumed you have the basic cooking skills required to make the most of leftovers and whip them into delicious dinners. Use your common sense with quantities and give these recipes a go. You can't go far wrong.

Remember The sell-by dates and best-before labels on food are about quality, not safety. But the use-by date is just that, so don't ignore it.

Lovely leftovers

We are all guilty of chucking away food that's past its best or binning the leftovers, so here are some delicious ways to cut back on waste.

BRILLIANT BREAD

It's easy to throw away bread once it's got a little stale, but our superscrimpers can think of dozens of uses for those remaining less-than-fresh slices.

THE AVERAGE PERSON IN THE UK SPENDS £439.30 EACH YEAR ON READY-MADE SANDWICHES.

Source: British Sandwich Association

Breadcrumbs

Finely grate stale bread into a bowl (or you can use a food processor, if you happen to have one). Tip the crumbs into a freezer bag and pop them in the freezer – use them straight from frozen in a crumble topping, or as a coating for fish. If your bread isn't dry enough to grate straight away, cut it into thin slices and dry it out in the oven on a low heat.

Another way to make the crumbs is to break the bread into pieces, place it in a plastic bag, seal it and then bash with a rolling pin. That'll soon get rid of the blues.

A giant toasted croûton

Bake a slice of stale bread in the oven at 180°C/350°F/gas mark 4
for 10–12 minutes until crisp and golden brown. Top with soup
or leftover stew, or cover with cheese and melt under the grill. For
a really tasty treat, rub a cut garlic clove over the bread before it goes
in the oven.

Fried croûtons

Cut the stale bread into cubes and fry in a little oil over a low
heat, turning so that they brown evenly. Drain on kitchen paper.
They'll keep in an airtight container for up to two weeks. Delicious
sprinkled over soup or salad.

Italian bread salad (*panzanella*)

This is a lovely recipe for a summer salad. The bread soaks up all the
lovely juices.

You will need:
stale bread
olive oil
dried herbs
*chopped summer salad ingredients, such as bell peppers,
cucumber and tomatoes*
olives, capers and basil
salt and pepper
vinaigrette

Cut the stale bread into chunks, coat in olive oil and then sprinkle generously with dried herbs. Fry in a pan or bake in the oven at 180°C/350°F/gas mark 4, until the bread is toasty and brown.

Put the bread in a big bowl and mix in the salad ingredients. Add the olives, capers and the basil. Season well and drizzle with a little vinaigrette.

French toast (or eggy bread)

A real breakfast treat – it's so luxurious, no one will ever know it's made from leftovers.

For 1 slice, you will need:
a slice of stale bread
1 egg
a splash of milk
sugar
ground cinnamon
a knob of butter, for frying

Remove the crusts from the bread. Break the egg into a bowl, add a splash of milk and beat well with a fork. Dip the bread into the eggy mixture, making sure it's completely covered.

Heat a shallow frying pan and melt a knob of butter then fry the eggy bread on both sides until golden brown.

Sprinkle with sugar and a little cinnamon and eat while still warm.

Bread and butter pudding

Bread and butter pudding is the queen of thrifty desserts. It's simple to make, costs pennies and tastes delicious.

To serve 6–8, you will need:
275ml milk
225g bread, torn into bits
175g dried fruit
75g margarine
25g Demerara sugar
1 tsp mixed spice
a little grated nutmeg
1 egg
a large splash of brandy
a squeeze of lemon or orange juice

Pour the milk over the bread and let it soak for half an hour.

Add the rest of the ingredients to the milky bread and mix together thoroughly. Spread evenly in a shallow pie dish and cook in the oven at 180°C/350°F/gas mark 4 for 1¾–2 hours.

Eat in big warm chunks.

Bread-basket canapés

Peas, beans and carrots seem unlikely ingredients for a dinner party canapé but with a little creative cookery they can be cheap and chic.

You will need:
stale sliced bread
butter, for spreading
pea purée, carrot paté filling or spicy cannellini bean mash (see below)

Cut the crusts off the bread and roll each slice out flat with a rolling pin. Butter both sides then ease the slices into a muffin tin and bake in a warm oven (180°C/350°F/gas mark 4) for 10 minutes until

crisp. Remove from
the oven and leave
to cool in the tins
so that they keep
their shape.
Once cool you
can fill your bread
baskets with any
of the following:

Pea purée

Blitz cooked peas,
fresh mint, sour
cream and seasoning
in a food processor
until smooth. Add
more sour cream
until you get the
right consistency.

Carrot pâté

Roast carrots in olive oil and fry a chopped onion with a little curry
paste. Blitz the whole lot in the food processor to make a delicious
carrot paté.

Spicy cannellini bean mash

Simmer a tin of cannellini beans until tender then mash them with
a finely chopped red chilli and some chopped spring onions. Stir
in cream cheese, a spoonful at a time, until it has a smooth texture.

THRIFTY IDEAS FOR LEFTOVER TATTIES

The humble potato has seen us through many a hungry evening when the cupboards are bare. Here are some tips for using up a glut.

- Slice and shallow fry leftover boiled potatoes in oil.

- Mash leftover potatoes with an egg and some flour, then shape into flat round patties. Fry to make potato cakes.

- Chop up cold spuds, mix with a dollop of mayonnaise and sprinkle on some tasty chopped parsley and chives for a swoonsome potato salad.

Ready-for-roasting potatoes

If you've got a whole bag of potatoes, peel and wash all the potatoes at once. Chop them in half and parboil for about 5 minutes. Drain and cool, then put them in freezer bags and freeze. They'll be perfect for roasties straight from the freezer – just toss them in hot oil in a roasting tin and cook in the oven as normal.

Herby mash sauce

People often throw away coriander and parsley stalks but they're a flavourful addition to this leftover mash sauce. Serve over fish or chicken.

You will need:
onion, peeled and finely chopped
garlic, peeled and finely chopped

coriander stalks, chopped

parsley stalks, chopped

leftover mash

hot water, milk or stock

lemon juice

salt and pepper

oil, for frying

Shallow fry the onion and garlic until soft and golden. Stir in the chopped coriander and parsley stalks and cook for 3–4 minutes.

Add your mash to the pan and cook over a gentle heat for a further 3–4 minutes. Pour in enough hot water, milk or stock to make a smooth sauce, stirring constantly, and season to taste with salt and pepper. Add a squeeze of lemon juice to finish.

Duchess potatoes

It's easy to make pretty Duchess potatoes with leftover mash. Simply spoon the mash into a piping bag and pipe large rosettes of potato on to a lined baking tray. Brush with a little beaten egg and pop into the freezer (still on their trays) until firm. Store in freezer bags in the freezer until you're ready to cook them.

For super-quick baked potatoes insert a metal skewer through each potato before you cook them in the oven. The metal acts as a heat conductor and the spuds will cook in half the time.

Transform leftover roasted vegetables from dinner into a pasta sauce. Put them in the food processor, season with salt and pepper, add a bulb of roasted garlic and blitz until smooth. Freeze and cook straight from frozen.

REWARDING RICE

There's always a little rice left in the pan, but rather than chucking it away, why not make it into something even more delicious tomorrow?

Risotto balls

Leftover risotto and stale bread can make a surprisingly tasty picnic or lunch-box treat.

You will need:

leftover risotto

breadcrumbs (see page 12)

1 egg, beaten

oil, for frying

kitchen paper

Roll the risotto into small balls and dip first in the beaten egg then roll in the breadcrumbs to coat. Shallow fry in hot oil and pat dry on kitchen paper.

Rice pudding

A fast and tasty pud made from leftover dinner rice. Quantities will vary depending how much rice you use. Just make sure you don't scrimp on the coconut milk so that your pudding is nice and creamy.

You will need:
leftover rice
coconut milk
sugar
lime zest, optional

Put the rice in a pan and add half to two-thirds of the coconut milk. Warm in a pan over a moderate heat. Stir in some sugar, to taste, and the lime zest, if using, and cook until the dessert is piping hot.

Rice won't keep for long but adding turmeric to the cooking water helps to preserve it. Cold rice is great for stir-frying because refrigeration stiffens the starchy outer layer of the grains. Simply add spring onions, peas and leftover chicken pieces to the pan with a splash of soy sauce and a dribble of honey for a quick lunch with an oriental twist.

BRILLIANT BIRDS

Most of us eat chicken at least once a week – it's quick, easy and healthy, but it can be expensive. Here are some tips for how to get more bird for your buck.

An easy chicken marinade

Half a jar of pesto lurking in the fridge? Check its use-by date; if it's fine, empty it into a mixing bowl. Add a sprinkle of salt and a squeeze of lemon juice and mix together. Pop chicken breasts in the mix and leave in the fridge for 2 hours, so that the flavours infuse. You can use this tasty marinade with other white meat or fish.

A spicy chicken marinade

This will add an exotic kick to your usual chicken dishes but at almost no cost.

To make enough to coat a chicken, you will need:

120ml lemon juice

2 tbsp chilli powder

1 dssp ground ginger

3 tbsp paprika

2 garlic cloves, peeled and crushed

Mix all the ingredients in a bowl and massage into your chicken. Leave in the fridge for at least 2 hours before cooking.

Chicken stock

The carcass of a roast can be turned into delicious stock. Put the parson's nose, skin and any other inedible bits in a pot. Then add half an onion, 1 litre of water, a pinch of salt, a grind of pepper and a bay leaf. Simmer until the stock is thick, strain and pour into an airtight container. Store in the fridge or freeze for later.

TURKEY LEFTOVERS

Turkey is cheaper than chicken and is seriously underrated. Using just a few store-cupboard ingredients, that looming leftover turkey can be turned into four family dinners. Just make sure the meat is properly cooked through.

Turkey risotto

Risotto has a reputation as a tricky dish to make, but the key is to stir often and add the stock slowly so that it has time to absorb. Follow these simple instructions and you'll be eating rich, creamy risotto Mama would be proud of in no time.

To serve 4, you will need:

1 litre chicken/turkey/vegetable stock (chop-bought or see pages 23 and 28)

2 tbsp olive or vegetable oil

1 onion, peeled and finely chopped

1 garlic clove, peeled and finely chopped

350g Arborio or Carnaroli rice

a good pinch of Chinese five spice

120ml dry white wine, optional

225g cooked turkey, chopped into bite-sized pieces

50g frozen peas

25g butter

25g grated Parmesan cheese

salt and pepper

Heat the stock in a saucepan and simmer gently.

Heat the oil in a frying pan, add the onion and sauté over a gentle heat for about 5 minutes until softened, then add the garlic. Stir in the rice and cook for a minute or so until the grains begin to look translucent and are coated in the oil.

Mix in the Chinese five spice, splash over the wine (if using) and stir until the wine stops sizzling and is absorbed by the rice.

Then add the stock to the rice, a ladleful at a time, allowing each ladleful to be absorbed before adding the next. After 15 minutes add the turkey and continue cooking until the rice is tender, then cook for a further 15 minutes. Add the frozen peas, butter and the Parmesan and stir well. Season, to taste, with salt and pepper.

Batch cooking is a great way to save energy and money. If you're cooking in the oven, but it's only half full, you're squandering heat. A better solution is to cook in batches, filling all the shelves. Cook in bulk and stock up the freezer.

Turkey-broccoli bake

This cheesy bake is just the thing for a cold winter's night.

To serve 2, you will need:
225g broccoli, cut into florets
50g grated cheese
50g breadcrumbs
1 x 400g tin of condensed mushroom soup
2 tbsp mayonnaise
2–3 tbsp single cream or milk
juice of ½ a lemon
225g cooked turkey, chopped into bite-sized pieces

Preheat the oven to 200°C/400°F/gas mark 6.

Blanch the broccoli in boiling water for a few minutes until just tender. Mix the grated cheese with the breadcrumbs.

Pour the mushroom soup into a bowl and add the mayonnaise and cream. Pour over the lemon juice. Add the chopped turkey and mix together. Layer the broccoli in a baking dish and spread the turkey mix over the top. Sprinkle the cheese and breadcrumbs over the whole dish and bake for 25–30 minutes, until golden brown and bubbling.

Turkey Provençal

This is a filling and delicious meal that can be served simply with some cooked rice. Turn up the heat by adding a teaspoon of chilli powder and a few chilli flakes or a tablespoon of curry paste to the softened onion and cook for 1 minute before adding the rest of the ingredients.

To serve 2, you will need:
1 onion, peeled and sliced
oil, for frying
5 mushrooms, sliced
150g cooked turkey, chopped into bite-sized pieces
1 x 400g tin of chopped tomatoes
a pinch of dried mixed herbs
2–3 tbsp natural yoghurt or cream, optional
salt and pepper

Fry the onion in a little oil until soft. Add the mushrooms, turkey and tomatoes. Add a pinch of salt, a good grind of pepper and a pinch of mixed herbs. Simmer for 10–15 minutes until the sauce is reduced. Stir in the yoghurt or cream, if you fancy.

• •

Coronation turkey

This turkey curry is best served cold with a crunchy salad, or as sandwich filling.

To serve 4, you will need:
1 small onion, peeled and chopped
4 ready-to-eat apricots, chopped into small pieces

1 tsp turmeric

zest and juice of 1 lemon

2 tbsp mild curry paste

2 tbsp mango chutney

1 tbsp tomato purée

4 tbsp dry white wine, optional

6 tbsp mayonnaise

2 tbsp double cream, crème fraîche or Greek yoghurt

300g cooked turkey, chopped into bite-sized pieces

salt and pepper

olive oil, for frying

Heat the oil in a frying pan, add the onion and fry over gentle heat for about 5 minutes until softened. Add the apricots, turmeric, lemon zest and juice, curry paste, mango chutney, tomato purée and wine (if using; if not, stir in 2 tablespoons of water) and simmer for 5 minutes until the sauce is the consistency of chutney. Take off the heat and leave to cool.

When cold, fold the mayonnaise and cream into the curry sauce then add the turkey pieces and mix until they are evenly coated. Season, to taste, and chill until required.

Turkey stock

Consign the carcass to a large saucepan. Add onions and carrots and let it bubble away for an hour. Drain, keeping all the liquid, but discarding the carcass and the vegetables. The rich stock can be used in soups and risottos.

MORE FROM YOUR MEAT

There are plenty of clever ways to use up leftover meat.

Pâté

The trimmings from leftover cooked meat can easily be made into a delicious pâté. Serve on crackers or hot toast.

You will need:

1 red onion, peeled and finely chopped
a knob of fresh ginger, finely chopped
1 garlic clove, peeled and finely chopped
½ tsp finely chopped green chilli
½ tsp ground turmeric
a pinch of red chilli powder
leftover meat, cut into pieces
salt
juice of ½ a lemon
single cream
cream cheese
butter, for frying

Melt a little butter in a pan and fry the onion until soft. Add the ginger, garlic and chilli. Sprinkle in the turmeric, chilli powder and meat. Add salt and a squeeze of lemon juice. Heat thoroughly.

While it's still hot, blend the mixture with a drizzle of fresh cream, a spoonful of cream cheese and a spoonful of butter – add more until you have the right consistency. Blend and chill in the fridge.

To make a mince recipe go further, add a couple of cups of porridge oats to the recipe. The oats will soak up the juices, and once all the flavour has been absorbed it'll taste just as good as the meat.

Mini pasties

Cooked leftover mince is an ideal filling for these mini pasties, and you can add to the mix whatever else you have lurking in the fridge – chopped carrots or onions are a good addition. Ready-made pastry is always a good standby to have in the fridge. It's inexpensive to buy or, even better, freeze leftover homemade pastry when you've made a little too much for your pie.

You will need:
leftover cooked mince
ready-made shortcrust pastry
flour, for dusting
a beaten egg

a round cookie cutter or a small glass

Preheat the oven to 200°C/400°F/gas mark 6.

Roll out the pastry on to a floured surface. Use a cookie cutter or small glass to press out pastry circles.

Spoon a little of the mince on to the circles, and then fold them into pasty shapes. Crimp the edges with a fork. Pop them on a lined baking tray, glaze with egg wash and bake for 25 minutes, until the pastry is golden and the filling is steaming hot.

Less costly cuts

Their names might not be very glamorous – kidneys, liver, beef shin, scrag end of lamb – but these cheaper cuts are delicious and very affordable.

Sweet and sour kidneys

Kidneys used to be very popular but in recent years they have fallen out of favour. It's time to bring back these tasty, healthy treats.

To serve 4, you will need:

2 tbsp honey

3 tbsp dry sherry

4 tbsp soy sauce

300ml beef stock (from stock cube)

1 garlic clove, peeled and crushed

a pinch of Chinese five spice

450g lambs' kidneys, halved and cored

25g plain flour

50g butter

1 tbsp cornflour

chopped parsley

salt and pepper

Mix together the honey, sherry, soy sauce, stock, garlic and Chinese five spice. Add the halved and cored kidneys and marinate for 1 hour. Remove the kidneys, reserving the marinade and pat dry.

Season the flour with salt and pepper and coat the kidneys with the flour. Melt the butter in a pan and fry the kidneys until just browned, then remove them from the pan. Add the marinade to the pan and bring to the boil.

Mix the cornflour with 1 tablespoon of water, then stir the mixture into the pan and cook until the sauce thickens. Return the kidneys to the pan, season to taste, and cook for 2–3 minutes until heated through. Stir in the chopped parsley before serving.

Hungarian goulash

This traditional stew will keep you warm and fill you up so you get twice the superscrimper points. The sauce is great with beef but works really well with mushrooms, too.

To serve 4, you will need:
750g beef shin
2 tbsp oil
2 onions, peeled and sliced
1 red pepper, deseeded and chopped
25g plain flour
2 tbsp paprika
2 x 400g tins of chopped tomatoes
500ml beef stock
bouquet garni
1 tsp dried thyme
salt and pepper
150ml soured cream or natural yoghurt, to serve
chopped parsley, to garnish

Sauté the meat in the oil in a large pan, then remove and set aside. Lower the heat and fry the onions and red pepper until soft. Add the flour and paprika. Stir for 1 minute and then add the tomatoes and stock and bring to a simmer, stirring continuously. Return the meat to the pan along with the bouquet garni and thyme and season with salt and pepper.

Transfer all the ingredients to an ovenproof casserole, cover and cook for 2½–3 hours at 160°C/325°F/gas mark 3. Remove the bouquet garni and divide between serving plates or bowls. Spoon a little cream on top of the goulash and garnish with parsley.

Irish stew

You can't beat a good stew and this is one of the best around. The slow cooking means this cheaper cut of meat becomes meltingly soft – in fact, it simply wouldn't work as well with a more expensive cut.

To serve 4, you will need:
750g scrag end neck of lamb, cut into chops
2 large onions, peeled and sliced
500–750g potatoes, peeled and sliced
450ml stock or water
salt and pepper
chopped parsley, to garnish

Pop the meat in a saucepan with the onions and half the potatoes. Add the water or stock and season with salt and pepper. Bring to boiling point and remove any 'scum' from the top. Cover with the lid, lower the heat and simmer gently for about 1½ hours.

Add the rest of the sliced potatoes to the stew and continue cooking for a further 40 minutes. Taste and add more seasoning if necessary. Ladle into warmed dishes and garnish with chopped parsley.

Liver and bacon parcels

These are sweet, comforting and cheap. What more could you ask for?

To serve 4, you will need:
450g lamb's liver, sliced
8 rashers of back bacon, chopped
2 onions, peeled and sliced
2 large potatoes, peeled and thinly sliced
1 tsp dried thyme
8 tbsp stock or water
salt and pepper
butter, for greasing

Line a baking tray with buttered foil. Pop the slices of liver on the foil.

Cover the liver with the bacon, onions and potatoes. Sprinkle over the thyme and season with salt and pepper. Spoon over the stock or water. Close the foil loosely over the ingredients and seal at the sides to make a parcel. Cook in the oven for 45 minutes at 200°C/400°F/gas mark 6. Remove from the foil to serve.

Making the most of what you've got

The bottom shelf of the fridge and back of the cupboard often harbour past-their-best odds and ends. Here are some tips to prevent fresh food from perishing quite so quickly.

50% OF LETTUCE BOUGHT IN THE UK IS WASTED

Source: Wrap, 2009

How to revive limp lettuce

Squeeze the juice of half a lemon into a bowl of cold water. Plunge the limp lettuce in and pop in the fridge for half an hour. Remove the bowl from the fridge and, hey presto, the lettuce is lovely again.

Simple salad dressing

When you reach the end of the goodies in a jar of antipasti, use the flavoured oil left in the bottom as a base for salad dressing. Just add a spoonful of mustard, a slug of honey, a splash of vinegar, a pinch of salt and a grind of pepper. Screw the lid back on the jar and give the dressing a good shake.

How to keep cut onions fresh

To stop the cut end of an onion drying out, rub a little butter over the exposed end, wrap the onion in foil and store in the fridge.

More spring in your onions

If your spring onions still have their roots, don't put them in the fridge; instead, pour about 2.5cm of water in a glass and pop the onions in it. Change the water every couple of days and you'll see the roots and the blades flourish. Most people only use the bulb of the spring onion, but the crunchy green blades are superb in salads and soups.

Broccoli and cauliflower stems

Sadly, these stems tend to get left behind on the chopping board. But, not only are they nutritious and delicious, you also buy these vegetables by weight, so by not making use of them you're throwing money away.

Cauliflower stems are tender enough to use as they are, but broccoli can be a bit tougher. Stand the broccoli stem upright and, using a paring knife, peel away the outer, woody layer. They make a fantastic addition to salads – although you can pop them in any dish where you are using the florets.

Making herbs last longer

Herbs can go off quickly, but a couple of sheets of kitchen towel can delay the rot. Take the herbs out of their plastic packets, rinse them and then shake off the excess water. Lay the herbs on a square or two of kitchen roll, and then roll up the herbs in the paper. Keep them in a clean plastic bag in the vegetable drawer of the fridge.

The kitchen roll will absorb the gases created by the herbs that speed up decay, and it will also regulate the moisture. Try adding a square of kitchen roll to bags of salad and inside the punnets of soft fruit to keep them fresher for longer.

Revive soft crackers

Soggy, soft crackers can be crisped up with a brief visit to the oven. Pop them on a baking tray and into a medium oven for a few minutes. Whip them out and their crispness will have been restored.

Get more from your teabag

Pop your teabag into an empty litre flask. Boil just enough water to fill the flask, and pour it in. Put the lid on and give it a quick shake, then leave the tea to infuse. You'll get three cups of tea from one teabag, and you save on electricity or gas.

How to keep your coffee

Coffee can get claggy at the bottom of a storage jar. Pop half a biscuit in the coffee tin – it'll soak up all the moisture, and save you 6–8 cups per jar.

Make juice go further

This solution is simple: dilution. Pour a slug of juice into a glass and top up with tap water. Better for your teeth, too.

Lemon and lime aid

Lemons are the multitaskers of the kitchen.

WITH A LEMON YOU CAN:

Revive lettuce

(see page 36)

Mix up a face mask

(see page 169)

Clean your nails

(see page 176)

Infuse limoncello

(see page 70)

Soften your hands

(see page 175)

Make a hairspray

(see page 166)

De-pong the fridge

(see page 81)

Descale the kettle

(see page 80)

Clean copper

(see page 85)

Get more lemon for your squeeze

Roll the lemon on the worktop until its soft before you cut and squeeze – you'll get twice as much juice.

If you only need a little drop of lemon juice, there's no need to squeeze the whole fruit. Insert a metal skewer into the end of the lemon, and squeeze out as much as you need. Wrap the lemon in foil and keep in the fridge. It will last for weeks, rather than days.

Leftover limes

Leftover limes can get very dry. If you know you're not going to use all the fruit, cut up the whole lime, pop the chunks into freezer bags and freeze. Gin and tonic, anyone? Pop a nice iced lime wedge in your drink.

PRESERVING THE PLEASURE

A surplus of fruit at the end of the season is a reason for celebration. Embrace the ancient art of preservation and you can enjoy the fruits of your labour all year round. Jammy!

Strawberry jam

Squishy over-ripe strawberries are just the thing for making jam.

To fill about 3 jars, you will need:
500g strawberries, roughly chopped
1 apple, roughly chopped
lemon juice
350g caster sugar

sterilized glass jars (see below)

Sterilise the jars by washing in very hot water or on the hot cycle in a dishwasher. Dry by placing in a preheated oven at 160°C/325°F/gas mark 3 for 10–15 minutes, then leave to cool.

Place the strawberries and apple in a hot pan with a squeeze of lemon juice. Add the sugar and simmer on the hob for 10 minutes. Once the mixture has cooled a little, pour into a sterilized jar and seal immediately.

A chutney using past-their-best tomatoes

A delicious addition to a cheese sandwich or a summer salad.

You will need:

1.4kg ripe tomatoes, chopped

450g apples, peeled, cored and roughly chopped

225g onions, peeled and sliced

400ml malt vinegar

225g brown sugar

225g sultanas

2 tsp salt

1 tsp mustard powder

2 tsp ground ginger

½ tsp cayenne pepper

3 tsp pickling spice

an old pair of clean tights (don't worry, all will become clear)

sterilized glass jars (see page 41)

Put the tomatoes, apples and onions in a large pan with the vinegar, sugar, sultanas, salt, mustard powder, ginger and the cayenne pepper.

Make a spice bag by cutting one foot off the old pair of tights – it should be the length of a sock. An easy way to get the spices in the tights is to stretch the foot over the top of a glass jar, leaving a little slack across the rims. Spoon in the pickling spices into the slack, roll the tights up around the spices and tie to secure the spices inside, then tie the tights around the handle of the pan and push the full end under the chutney liquid. Bring to the boil, then simmer uncovered for 2 hours until the mixture has reduced and thickened. Discard the pickling spice-filled tights and leave to cool. Store in sterilized jars and seal at once.

Fruit chutney

Soft pears and bruised apples cut into chunks make excellent chutney.

You will need:
apples, peeled and cored
pears , peeled and cored
fennel seeds, crushed
cardamom seeds, crushed
onion, peeled and chopped
sugar
malt vinegar
mixed spice or garam masala
a little oil for frying

sterilized glass jars (see page 41)

Chop the fruit into bite-sized pieces. Drizzle a little oil into a pan and fry the crushed fennel and cardamom seeds with the chopped onion. Add the chopped fruit and cook for 5–8 minutes.

Sprinkle over some sugar and continue cooking until the sugar dissolves and the liquid evaporates. Add a splash of malt vinegar and, as a final touch, add mixed spices or garam masala. Spoon the chutney into a glass dish and leave to cool, then transfer to sterilized glass jars and leave to mature for a month.

Better than bought

Branded products can cost a pretty penny, but it's easy to make some of your favourite foods at home, and much cheaper, too.

DIY DAIRY

Homemade butter and cheese sounds very impressive but it's actually a cinch to make.

Homemade butter

If you've got some cream that's nearing its use-by date, turn it into butter. Pour the cream into a clean glass jar, leaving a little room at the top. Shake the jar energetically and after a few minutes you'll notice a change in sound as the cream firms up. It'll sound sloshy because the buttermilk is separating from the butter. Drain away the buttermilk, add some clean water to the jar and gently rock and roll it to wash out more of the buttermilk. Strain again. Repeat a few times, until the water runs clear. Tip the butter out and squeeze out the rest of the moisture with a wooden spoon or paddle. And there you have it, homemade butter.

Cottage cheese

This scrimping recipe for cottage cheese will cost you pennies rather than pounds. For a creamier cheese stir two tablespoons double cream into the cheese at the end.

You will need:
1 litre full-fat milk
a good pinch of salt
3–4 tbsp something acidic – lemon juice, lime juice or vinegar.

muslin cloth

Warm the milk with a good pinch of salt in a saucepan over a low heat, stirring occasionally. Heat until the milk is steaming, but just below boiling point, then take the pan off the heat. Add in a splash of lemon juice, lime juice or vinegar. (This starts off a chemical reaction, which separates the protein from the whey.) Line a bowl with muslin and press the mixture through it with a spoon. The solids left in the bowl are cottage cheese.

Shape extra cottage cheese into balls and preserve it in oil. Flavour the oil with herbs and spices for added interest.

SIMPLE SAUCES

Shop-bought sauces cost a fortune and they're often full of salt and other nasties. Here are some simple sauces you can whip up at home.

Homemade tomato sauce

If you make a big batch, you can freeze it, and then when you reheat it, add in anything else you have hanging around that needs using up, like spinach leaves, mushrooms or olives.

To serve 4–6, you will need:

2 tbsp olive oil
450g tomatoes, roughly chopped
2 garlic cloves, peeled and finely chopped
½ tsp sugar
a glug of vinegar
salt and pepper

Heat the oil in a saucepan, add the tomatoes and garlic and bring to the boil. Add the sugar, vinegar, and season generously with salt and pepper. Simmer for about 15 minutes.

Frugal foraging

If you're feeling adventurous, you can use the great outdoors as your greengrocers. Lots of common plants are edible: dandelions are fine in a salad, young hawthorn leaves are great in a cheese sandwich. Even weeds can be treats: nettles and goose grass are a good substitute for spinach – just wilt them and add them to soups.

There are a few rules to follow while you search for your supper:

- Be respectful. Don't take too much of anything and make sure you leave the plant looking healthy so that it continues growing and you can re-visit years hence.

- Always, always check the identification of the plants and make sure they're 100 per cent edible. Use the App at www.foragesapp.com for reference, or check websites like www.eatweeds.co.uk.

- Some plants are protected species so make sure you're not breaking the law.

BON APPETIT

Nettle pasta

Hedgerows, field verges and untamed areas of the common are home to the common nettle. Fresh, young plants are the best. Always wear gloves to avoid being stung and pick the leaves towards the top of the plant, as these are tender and tastier.

To serve 2, you will need:
120g nettles
170g flour
2 eggs
1 tsp olive or sunflower oil
salt and pepper

Wash the nettles in hot water to remove the sting then finely chop and put in a bowl with the flour and eggs yolks. Season with a pinch of salt and a little pepper and mix together to form a dough.

Knead the dough on a floured surface then roll out and cut into thin strips with a flour-dusted knife (to stop the dough sticking). Leave the strips to rest in the fridge for 5 minutes then pop them into a pan of boiling water for 5 minutes. Drain and serve with homemade tomato sauce (see page 46).

Wild garlic pesto

Wild garlic is nearly impossible to buy in the shops, but it grows profusely near rivers, on bog land and in shady places (you'll never find it in a field). It's part of the onion family, has beautiful flowers, a tell-tale pungent garlic smell, and you can pick it from March to May. It can be used in salads, as a garnish, or in this delicious pesto.

You will need:

a good handful of wild garlic

a handful of grated Parmesan cheese

a handful of pine nuts (these are expensive and so can be replaced with walnuts or pumpkin seeds to keep costs down)

150ml olive oil

salt and pepper

sterilized glass jars (see page 41)

Put all the ingredients in a food processor, season with salt and pepper and whizz until you get a pesto consistency. Scrape the mixture into sterilized jars. It will keep in the fridge for about a month, or you can freeze it and enjoy wild garlic pesto throughout the year.

See also our recipes for foraged drinks on pages 69–73.

Canny ketchup

Once you've tried this, you'll never go back to the squeezy bottle.

To fill 1 ice-cube tray, you will need:

6 tomatoes, cut into eighths
½ tbsp salt
150ml white vinegar
a pinch of allspice
a pinch of ground cloves
a pinch of cayenne pepper
a pinch of cinnamon

strainer
ice-cube trays

Don't waste that last little dribble of ketchup: add some vinegar to the bottle and give it a good shake. Pop it in gravy for a dash of extra zip, flavoured by the satisfaction that you've not wasted a penny.

Put the chopped tomatoes in a pan with the salt and vinegar. Simmer for half an hour until the tomatoes have softened. Push the tomatoes through a strainer with a spoon, and then return to the hot pan. Stir in the spices. Put the pan back on the heat, until the tomatoes thicken like ketchup. Cool then freeze individual portions in ice-cube trays until needed.

Cheap 'n' cheerful cheese sauce

A perfect sauce for chicken or fish. Make as much or as little as you need and adjust the quantities to fit.

You will need:
onion, peeled and chopped

garlic, peeled and chopped
milk or coconut milk
hard cheese (like Cheddar)
black pepper
freshly chopped coriander, for garnishing
a little oil, for frying

Fry the onion and garlic in a little oil until they're soft. Add the milk or coconut milk and simmer for a few minutes to thicken slightly. Grate the cheese into the milk and stir to mix together. It should have a good sauce consistency so add more cheese or milk as needed. Grind over a twist of black pepper and sprinkle with freshly chopped coriander.

Simple white sauce

This is a really simple base sauce to which you can add flavours such as herbs, spices, or even sugar or honey (omitting the seasoning). The secret is to blend the flour and fat first before adding the liquid.

You will need:
30g margarine, melted
30g flour
½ pint warm milk or vegetable stock
salt and pepper

In a saucepan over a medium heat, stir the flour into the melted margarine. Heat until the mixture bubbles and spreads then remove from the heat. Add the milk gradually, stirring constantly and return to the heat to thicken. Once thickened allow to simmer for at least 5 minutes. Season and flavour with whatever you have to hand.

The ice-cube tray

Any number of leftover liquids can be poured into ice-cube trays and frozen for perfectly portioned use later on.

- Don't let a half-used jar of pesto go mouldy in the fridge, instead spoon the leftover sauce into ice-cube trays, and freeze. When you need a basil boost for a dish just add a pesto cube.

- Pour leftover gravy into ice-cube trays and freeze it, then it's on hand to add a dash of richness to stocks and sauces.

- If there's any wine left in the bottom of the bottle, pour it into an ice-cube tray and freeze. Use a couple of cubes when you want to pep up spaghetti bolognese or a pasta sauce.

- Chop up leftover herbs and pack them into ice cube trays. Pour a little water over the top and freeze. You can mix and match the herbs, or keep each cube just one variety. Use them as a flavour boost in soups, sauces and drinks.

Prudent puds and brilliant bakes

Indulge in a tasty treat with these delicious cakes and de-lovely desserts. And, even sweeter, they won't break the bank!

Over-ripe banana muffins

Don't be tempted to bin bruised, squidgy bananas. Instead, bake them into these marvellous muffins.

To make 12, you will need:

2 eggs
125ml vegetable oil
250g plain flour
100g caster sugar
½ tsp bicarbonate of soda
1 tsp baking powder
3 very ripe bananas, mashed
150g white chocolate chips

12 muffin cases
muffin tray

Preheat the oven to 200°C/400°F/gas mark 6. Line the muffin tray with the muffin cases.

In a bowl beat the eggs into the oil. In another, bigger bowl, mix the dry ingredients together and add the oil and egg mixture. Spoon in the mashed banana and fold in the chocolate chips. Divide the mix between the muffin cases and bake in the preheated oven for 20 minutes.

. . . .

Banana loaf

Who doesn't love a banana loaf? And this is one recipe that actually benefits from slightly overripe fruit.

To make a 1 loaf, you will need:
200g self-raising flour
a pinch of salt
100g butter
1 banana, mashed
2 eggs, beaten
½ tbsp mixed spice
100g mixed peel
50g walnuts

a lined loaf tin

Preheat the oven to 180°C/350°F/gas mark 4. Sieve the flour into a bowl and add a little salt. Rub in the butter, then add the mashed banana and the beaten eggs. Add in the rest of ingredients and mix gently to combine. Pour into a lined loaf tin and cook for about an hour and 10 minutes, until an inserted skewer comes out clean.

Heart jam tarts

These simple jam tarts are a great way of using up leftover jam or pastry.

To make about 18 small tarts, you will need:
225g plain flour, plus extra for dusting
a pinch of salt
1 tbsp icing sugar
110g butter
jam
vanilla sugar, for dusting (see below)

a round cookie cutter
a heart-shaped cookie cutter a bit smaller than the round cutter
cupcake tin

Preheat your oven to 180°C/350°F/gas mark 4. Dust a work surface with a little flour.

Sieve the flour, salt and icing sugar into a bowl. Using your fingers, mix in the butter until the mixture resembles breadcrumbs. Add cold water, one tablespoon at a time, until you've made a nice dough.

Roll the dough out on to your floured surface, until it's 0.5cm thick. Cut out circles from the dough and put them into a greased cupcake tin. Spoon in the jam. Cut out heart shapes from the leftover pastry and place one on top of each tart. Pop the tarts in the oven and bake for 15 minutes. Remove them from the oven, dust with some vanilla sugar and leave to cool.

VANILLA SUGAR is delicious and comes with a costly price tag, but it can be made cheaply at home. Put a vanilla pod into a jar of caster sugar, pop the lid on and let it infuse for a couple of weeks. The sugar will take on the flavour of the vanilla pod.

Luxury mince pies

Add brandy to cheap mincemeat for a dash of luxury. Instead of a pastry topping for the pies, use macaroon mix instead.

To make 6 pies, you will need:
1 x 400g jar of mincemeat
a glug of brandy
110g plain flour
50g fat (a mix of 25g of butter and 25g of margarine makes the best pastry)
2 large egg whites
100g ground almonds
25g ground rice
175g caster sugar
a few drops of almond essence
browned flaked almonds for decorating, optional

a round cookie cutter
12 cupcake or muffin cases
a cupcake baking tray

Preheat the oven to 190°C/375°F/gas mark 5. Add a glug of brandy to your mincemeat, give it a mix and set aside.

Mix the flour, butter, margarine and a splash of cold water to make a pastry dough. Roll out on to a lightly floured surface and cut out twelve circles. Line your cupcake tin with the pastry circles and spoon mincemeat into each one.

For the macaroon topping, beat the egg whites until they're very stiff, then carefully fold in the almonds, rice and sugar. Add a few drops of almond essence. Spoon the macaroon mix generously on to the pies, completely covering the mincemeat. Then sprinkle over the flaked almonds, if using. Bake for 25–30 minutes, until lightly brown.

Evaporated milk jelly

This is a classic dessert from the post-war era. Serve it in an elegant glass bowl for maximum nostalgia.

To serve 2, you will need:
1 x 170ml tin of evaporated milk
135g jelly
a squeeze of lemon

Chill the tin of evaporated milk in the fridge for a minimum of 2 hours – and better still, leave it overnight.

Into a saucepan pop the jelly, a little water and a good squeeze of lemon juice, and dissolve over a low heat. While it's dissolving beat the evaporated milk in a blender. Trickle the melted jelly slowly into the milk, blending as you go. Decant into a glass bowl and chill in the fridge for a couple of hours to firm up.

Ice lollies

Pour 200ml cheap lemonade into a jug and add a couple of drops of blue food colouring (or whatever shade takes your fancy). Stir and pour into mini ice-cream moulds. If you haven't got moulds, yoghurt pots and sticks will do the job just as well. Freeze for 6–8 hours. The ice lollies are lovely and fizzy, and as an added bonus they'll turn your tongue blue.

• •

Chocolate lollies

Spoon dollops of melted chocolate on to baking parchment, smooth out a little and put a lolly stick in the middle of each one. Sprinkle with hundreds and thousands and refrigerate for 30 minutes to set.

Delectable edible gifts

Homemade gifts bring pleasure to both the giver and the receiver. There's nothing better than a present that's been lovingly made and carefully packaged by hand. And these edible treats are sure to satisfy even the hardest to please.

Ladybird biscuits

Go dotty for these spotty, easy-to-make treats. Make as much, or as little, as you like.

You will need:

red food colouring

white icing

shop-bought digestive biscuits

melted chocolate and chocolate buttons, to decorate

a piping bag

Mix a few drops of red food colouring into a tub of white icing.

Lay the digestives out on a flat surface and spread each one with the red icing. Leave to set.

Decorate each biscuit with piped melted chocolate and buttons in the shape of a ladybird for the perfect children's party treat.

Stained-glass cookies

The boiled sweet at the heart of these cookies melts as the cookie bakes. When it cools down, hold it up to the light and it looks like a stained glass. Make a hole at one edge and you can hang them on the Christmas tree.

To make about 12 biscuits, you will need:

350g plain flour,
1 tsp bicarbonate of soda
½ tsp salt
1 tsp ground ginger
1 tsp cinnamon
½ tsp grated nutmeg
110g butter
100g golden caster sugar
75g soft brown sugar
1 egg
3 tbsp golden syrup
brightly coloured boiled sweets

Don't waste the pastry you cut from your cookies – miniature cookie-bites make perfect canapés.

cookie cutters, various sizes
drinking straw or skewer and ribbon, if you want to hang up the cookies

Preheat your oven to 180°C/350°F/gas mark 4.

Mix together all the dry ingredients apart from the sugar, then rub in the butter slowly until the mixture resembles breadcrumbs. Stir in the sugar. Beat the egg and syrup together with a fork then pour into the flour mixture. Knead until it comes together into a dough. Wrap in cling film or pop in a Tupperware container and leave to rest in the fridge for at least 20 minutes – the longer the better.

Roll out your rested dough on to a lightly floured surface then use a cutter to cut out the cookies. Place on a lined baking tray. Cut out the centre of each cookie with a smaller cookie cutter (no larger than 2cm wide) and pop a boiled sweet in the hole that's left. If you want to hang the cookies on the tree, carefully poke a hole in the top of each cookie. Bake in the oven for around 10 minutes.

When you take the cookies out of the oven, don't take them off the tray straight away. Once cooled, gently life the cookies from the tray and thread ribbon or string through the hole.

Honeycomb

Tempting as it is to marvel at the volcanic nature of making this crunchy treat, don't. Keep stirring, or else instead of honeycomb in a cake tin you'll have lava all over the kitchen.

You will need:
4 tbsp golden syrup
200g caster sugar
3 tsp bicarbonate of soda

greased 20cm-square
* cake tin*

Get those last golden drops of syrup by popping the glass jar of golden syrup in the microwave for a few seconds. Don't put a tin in; this will lead to a dangerous, messy disaster.

Put the golden syrup and sugar in a pan, stir and bring to the boil. Simmer for 5–10 minutes. Take off the heat and add the bicarbonate of soda. Stir vigorously for a few seconds Pour immediately into the cake tin. Leave to set and then have fun smashing your honeycomb into bite-sized pieces.

Handmade marzipan chocolates

Boxes of chocolates can be very expensive to buy, but cheap to make. Gather some extravagant edible decorations and get creative.

You will need:

1 x 500g block marzipan
100g dark chocolate, for dipping
Smarties (or other sweets), crystallized rose petals, walnuts, edible glitter, for decorating
toothpicks

Cut the marzipan into cubes. Melt the chocolate in the microwave, or in a glass bowl over a simmering saucepan of water.

Pierce a marzipan square with a cocktail stick and dip it in the melted chocolate so that the square is completely covered. Transfer the chocolate-covered squares to a sheet of baking parchment. Smooth over the chocolate with the cocktail stick and then decorate with a sprinkling of chopped nuts, Smarties or crystallized rose petals; add a touch of sparkle with edible glitter.

Leave your chocolates to set then wrap them in a square of cellophane (you can buy this from the garden centre) and tie with a riotous ribbon.

• •

Peppermint creams

Such a childhood classic and effortlessly easy to make. Adjust the mintiness to your preference.

You will need:

large egg white, beaten

225g icing sugar
peppermint essence
food colouring, optional

cookie cutter

Sieve 170g of the sugar into the beaten egg white and mix together. Slowly sieve in the rest of the sugar until you have a stiff paste. Mix in a few drops of peppermint essence. On a lightly sugared surface knead until the paste is smooth. Have a nibble. If it's not minty enough add more peppermint. Roll it out until it's about 0.5cm thick. Cut out the sweets with a cookie cutter, and leave to set.

Chocolate vodka

You can use ordinary plain or milk chocolate for this, but Mars bars, After Eights, or segments of Terry's Chocolate Orange will add a whole new flavour dimension.

To fill a 1-litre bottle, you will need:
200g chocolate, broken into pieces
150ml cream
400ml vodka

sterilized glass bottles (see instructions for sterilized jars, page 41)

Melt the chocolate in a bowl over a pan of hot water, making sure the bowl doesn't touch the water. When the chocolate has melted, stir in the cream. Remove from the heat, add the vodka and stir well. Pour into sterilized bottles and it's ready to drink, or add a pretty label, a bow and give away to friends.

Economical entertaining

Watching the purse strings doesn't mean you can't have people round to celebrate; you just have to be a bit clever with your canapés.

Mini luxury mince pies

Make mini pies for handing round with drinks by using petit fours cases instead of cupcake cases. Follow the recipe on page 56 but reduce the cooking time to 20 minutes and the cooking temperature to 180°C/350°F/gas mark 4.

Bite-sized banoffee pies

Tiny banoffee pies look good, taste even better and are much cheaper than a large, shop-bought version.

For 24 pies, you will need:

24 mini pastry cases
1 x 400g tin caramel
2 large bananas, chopped
300ml whipping cream
24 almonds

Scoop a spoonful of caramel into cooled pastry cases, top with chopped banana. Dollop on some whipped cream, and garnish each little pie with an almond.

Cheesy nibbles

These are great served with a glass of homemade bubbly (see page 72) and they are also a clever way of using up that leftover lump of cheese that's beginning to go hard.

To make 24 nibbles, you will need:
75g butter
110g plain flour
50g strong cheese
1 egg, separated
sesame seeds, optional
salt and pepper

5cm-diameter cookie cutter

Preheat the oven to 190°C/375°F/gas mark 5. Rub together the butter and flour in a bowl. Grate in the flavourful cheese. Add the egg yolk and mix the ingredients into a soft dough. Roll the dough out quite thinly on to a lightly floured surface then press out neat little rounds with the cookie cutter. Place on a lined baking tray, brush each biscuit with the egg white and sprinkle with the sesame seeds, if using. Bake for about 7–10 minutes, until lightly golden.

Cheese canapés

Fun to make and extremely decadent, no one will ever know you're watching the pennies. Adjust the quantities according to the number of guests.

You will need:
ready-roll puff pastry

chutney

cubes of assorted cheeses

1 egg, beaten

a cookie cutter or small glass

Roll out the puff pastry on to a lightly floured surface until it's about 1cm thick. Cut out pastry circles with a cookie cutter and arrange them on a lined baking tray. Prick the middle of each circle with a fork, so that it won't rise when baking. Spoon a little chutney into the middle of each circle and top with a couple of cubes of cheese – any variety will taste good. Glaze the edges of the pastry with the beaten egg. Bake at 200°C/400°F/gas mark 6 for 10–15 minutes, until the cheese has melted and the pastry has risen.

Tips for sophisticated soirées

Budget entertaining doesn't have to lack style. Brighten up your dinner-party table with these cute suggestions.

Cute cutlery

- Tear two pages out of an old book. Fold the top edge of one of the pages down about 2.5cm, as though you were folding down a bed sheet, and glue to fix. Glue together the sides of the unfolded sheet and stick the folded sheet on top. Pop a knife, fork and spoon into their paper beds.

- Bundle your cutlery together and tie ribbon and lace around them in a dashing bow.

Dessert display

- Teacups or espresso glasses are an elegant way to serve mousses or custards.

- Wine glasses are brilliant for trifle: start with a layer of jam, sprinkle on crushed amaretti biscuits (or digestives or ginger nuts), spoon over some mousse, add more biscuits and even more mousse.

Cut-price cocktails

Low cost doesn't mean missing out on the finer things in life. Banish those ruinous bar bills by mixing up your own cocktails and creating lavish drinks using supermarket own-brand spirits and hedgerow fruits and blooms. That way you can still have (elderflower) champagne on a lemonade budget. Bottoms up!

Blackberry liqueur

Juicy, freshly picked blackberries work best here, but you can also use frozen berries in this fruity liqueur.

For 2 x 1 litre bottles, you will need:

300g blackberries
450g granulated sugar
500ml cheap vodka

2 x 1 litre sterilized glass bottles (see instructions for sterilized jars, page 41)

Mash the berries with the sugar. Sterilize the concoction by bringing the fruity, sugary mixture to the boil either on the hob or in the microwave. Strain the mixture through a sieve and leave to cool. It should look syrupy, so add 500ml water and the vodka. Give it a good stir. Decant into sterilized bottles.

You can drink this liqueur straightaway but the longer you leave it the more flavourful and alcoholic it will become.

Irish cream

A rich treat with a less than ritzy price tag.

For a 1 litre bottle, you will need:

240ml condensed milk

240ml double cream

240ml whiskey

1 tsp instant coffee

1 tsp vanilla extract

1 x 1 litre sterilized glass bottle (see instructions for jars, page 41)

Put all the ingredients in a blender. Whizz for 30 seconds and decant into the sterilized bottle.

• •

Limoncello

A lemony holiday favourite that you can now make and enjoy at home.

For a 1 litre bottle, you will need:

750ml cheap vodka

zest and juice of 8 lemons

450g sugar

1 x 1 litre sterilized glass bottle (see instructions for jars, page 41)

Put the vodka and the lemon juice and zest in a large bowl.

Dissolve the sugar in 500ml water in a saucepan over a low heat. Pour the sugar syrup into the vodka and lemons. Cover the bowl and leave in a cool place for 5 days for the flavour to infuse Strain and pour into sterilized bottles.

Sloe gin

Pick some sloes from the hedgerows and make this lovely-to-look-at and delicious-to-sip drink.

For a 1 litre bottle, you will need:
450g sloes
225g caster sugar
1 litre cheap gin

1 x 1 litre sterilized glass bottle (see instructions for jars, page 41)

Prick the sloes with a pin, as they tend to be quite hard, then drop them into a sterilized glass bottle. Funnel in the sugar and top with gin. Seal with an airtight lid. Give it a shake then store in a cool, dark place. Once a week give the bottle another shake. In a couple of months you'll have sloe gin.

Elderflower champagne

The first hint that summer is on its way is the blooming of the elderflower. It looks lovely, but the flowers can also be made into champagne. Pick in May, and look for heads where some of the flowers are still unopened, so you know they're at their freshest. Don't pick them after rain showers or when they're still wet, as there may be some fungal spores nestling in the flowers. These spores could encourage mould to form in your champagne.

For a 1 litre bottle, you will need:
5 or 6 elderflower heads
2 lemons, sliced
750g caster sugar

2 tbsp cider vinegar

a 1 litre plastic bottle

Submerge the elderflower heads in 4.5 litres water in a big bowl. Shake off the flowers before you put them in the water, but don't wash them, as you want to make sure that the natural yeasts are still present to work their alcohol magic. Add the lemons and cover with a tea towel. Leave it to steep for 36–48 hours.

Strain the steeped solution through a sieve. Add the sugar and vinegar to the strained liquid. Stir to make sure that all the sugar has dissolved. Pour the liquid into plastic bottles and close the lids lightly, making sure not to close them fully. As your champagne starts to ferment, the yeast will expand the bottle, so you'll need to come back every couple of days and unscrew the lid to release the pressure. In three weeks you will have classy elderflower champagne to toast the summer sunshine. Cheers.

Mojito

To make the crushed ice for this refreshing cocktail, wrap ice cubes in a tea towel and bash them with a rolling pin.

Drop chopped limes into a glass and spoon in some sugar plus 6–10 fresh mint leaves. Crush together with a spoon to mix the flavours. Add crushed ice and a shot of rum and stir.

Pimms

Pimms is a delicious and economical party drink. Simply chop up oranges, strawberries, limes and cucumbers and put the fruit in a large jug. Put 3 or 4 large shots of Pimms in the jug and top up with lemonade.

SPICK AND SPAN HOME

WE SPEND A WHOPPING £1 BILLION EVERY YEAR ON CLEANING PRODUCTS IN THE UK.

But you don't have to spend a fortune on expensive, branded items. It's easy to be a diva with a duster using everyday ingredients. Load up your basket of tricks with:

BAKING POWDER

BICARBONATE OF SODA

OLD TOOTHBRUSHES

LEMONS

CLOTHS
– and you don't even have to buy these, as old soft T-shirts are perfect (you could even use old pants, but wash them first)

Brilliant bicarbonate of soda

Bicarbonate of soda is a fizzing wizard. With it you can:

Make china sparkle (see page 82)

Cut through the grime on an oven door (see page 80)

De-pong a smelly sink (see page 98)

Freshen up a carpet (see page 101)

Help put the fizz in bath bombs (see page 184)

Make honeycomb cookery like a science experiment (see page 61)

A sparkling kitchen

A grubby worktop is a real no no. Here's how to spruce up your cooking surfaces with just a few pence.

An all-purpose cleaning fluid

A good cleaning solution in the fight against grime can be made from one part vinegar, two parts water and a squeeze of lemon juice. This will clean pretty much any surface – bath, floor and kitchen cupboards included. Wash the windows with it and then dry the glass with old newspaper.

Scourers

Save the nets from your supermarket oranges and lemons. Put one net inside the other, and scrunch it up and you've got a free scouring pad.

Soap pads

An easy way to make a soap-filled pad go further is to cut it in half – two pads for the price of one.

Cut through the grease

Facing up to a sink full of dirty, greasy dishes? Add washing-up liquid as usual, but then add a couple of spoonfuls of white vinegar to the water. It'll cut through the grease like magic.

Saucepan cleaner

Remove burnt-on stains from pans with cheap cola. Pour in just enough of the drink to cover the burnt area. Boil, stir, then remove from the heat and pour away the cola and the burnt residue with it. Finish off with a quick wipe with a clean cloth.

Banish cooking smells

Boil a cup of vinegar with a few cloves in a saucepan for 2 minutes and any lingering cooking smells will disappear.

Descale the kettle

To get rid of limescale, put chunks of lemon in the kettle. Add water and boil, then leave it to stand over night.

Clean the oven

To get rid of burnt-on grime from a glass oven door, mix up a thick paste of bicarbonate of soda with a tiny amount of water. Lay some old newspaper on the floor underneath the oven door and, wearing rubber gloves, use a cloth to rub the paste on to the inside of the door. Leave it for about 15 minutes, then wash it off. The magic bicarbonate paste will also remove the remains of burnt food from the hob.

Clean the microwave

Boil a cup of hot water in the microwave. Pour the water into a bowl and add half a cup of lemon juice. Pop it in the microwave

for 30 seconds, take the bowl out and then give the oven a good
wipe down with a damp cloth.

Dishwater maintenance

A quick and easy way to keep your dishwasher in tip-top condition
is to give the sprinklers a good clean. Take them out and scrub them
with lemon juice and an old toothbrush. This will dislodge mould
and the residue of trapped food – the exact kind of debris that clogs
up the machine.

Three tips that will banish nasty niffs from the fridge

- Put a little bowl of bicarbonate of soda in the back of the
  fridge, it will absorb any lingering food smells.

- Halve a lemon and squeeze out the juice. (Freeze the juice
  to use later.) Cut the base off the squeezed half, to give in
  a nice flat end. Fill it with table salt and pop it in the fridge.

- Hide half an unpeeled potato in the fridge.

A polished property

Bring back the sparkle and shine with these simple cleaning solutions.

Cut glass

Crystal or cut glass can get very cloudy if it's washed in the dishwasher. For gleaming results hand wash in warm, soapy water, then dunk in a bowl with a solution of vinegar and water. Leave to air dry and then buff with a soft, clean cloth. Crystal clear.

China

Wipe stains from china with a little bit of bicarbonate of soda and a wet cloth. If the stains are really persistent, dissolve a denture-cleaning tablet in a bowl of water and soak the china in it. Rinse well.

Light switches

Use an ordinary rubber to erase grubby fingerprints around light switches.

Grotty grouting

Thick bleach and an old toothbrush will get grubby grouting glowing. Dip the toothbrush in the bleach, and use it to scrub between the tiles. Wipe down the surface with a damp cloth.

Furniture polish

The juice from half a lemon mixed with quarter of a cup of olive oil makes a great polish for wooden furniture. The lemon cuts through the grease, and the oil adds a lustrous shine.

Cleaning silver

There's no need to invest in silver cleaner to give this precious metal a lovely shine, you can banish the tarnish with any number of household products. Once it's clean, if you're not going to be using the silver straight away, wrap it in cling film, as this will protect it from the air and keep the tarnish away.

- Buy the cheapest toothpaste you can find and, using an old toothbrush, liberally coat the tarnished silver with the paste. Rinse and the tarnish will have vanished.

- Scrape all the white pith away from the inside of a banana skin. Wrap the peel around your finger so the inside is on the outside, then rub it all over the tarnished silver. Rinse with tap water and dry with a dishcloth.

- Dab methylated spirits on to a cotton wool pad and give the tarnished metal a good rub. Buff with a soft cloth.

Brass cleaner

In a small container, mix equal quantities of salt, flour and vinegar to a paste. Dab an old toothbrush into the paste, and apply it thickly to dingy brass. Leave on for at least an hour – the longer you leave it the shinier the metal will be. Wipe off the paste with a damp cloth and then buff with a dry, soft cloth.

· ·

Copper cleaner

Pour lemon juice on to the cloudy copper then sprinkle with salt. Rub the solution in with an old rag until the metal is gleaming again.

· ·

Wood cleaner

Coffee will get rid of scratches on dark wood. Take a spoonful of instant coffee, and pour on the tiniest amount of boiling water – the mixture should look like a strong espresso. Dip a clean cloth in the coffee and apply it to the scratches on the dark wood. When they've disappeared, buff with a clean dry cloth.

· ·

Wood polish

Pour half a bottle of baby oil into an empty spray bottle. Add in two generous squeezes of lemon juice. Put the lid back on the bottle and give it a shake. Spray on to the wood, let it soak in for a couple of minutes, and then go to work with a cloth.

Ceiling mould

A small patch of mould on the ceiling can be removed with diluted bleach. Make sure you wear gloves, goggles and a mask. Dilute 50ml bleach in 1 litre of water and rub away the mould. For large patches, call in a professional to discover the underlying cause.

Rust remover

WD40 and a scouring pad will work wonders on rust. Spray the WD40 on to the rusty surface and then apply a little elbow grease and the scourer. Use an old tea towel to dust always the rusty residue.

Rusty steel

Rusty steel can be revived with aluminium foil. Scrunch it up, wet it and rub it on to the rust – this works best on superficial damage. When you've finished scrubbing, wipe down the surface with an old, clean cloth.

Chrome polish

A dab of baby oil on a cloth will clean up chrome. Rub it in, and then polish.

Lovely laundry

Nothing smells more homely than freshly washed laundry. Here's how to get the most from your load.

A smelly washing machine

If your washing machine smells less than pleasant, put it on its hottest setting, but don't put in any washing powder or liquid detergent, or clothes. Let it run through its cycle. The hot water will kill the odours, and clean out the pipes, too.

Make your own washing powder

It's cheaper than shop-bought powder, and it's also better for the environment. When it comes to washing, add half a cup to your machine. If you've got the lid of an old hairspray can, scoop the mixture into that and pop it straight into the drum of the washing machine.

You will need:
1 x 125g bar of vegetable oil-based soap
250g soda crystals
20 drops essential oil

Heat 500ml water in a very large pan, until it boils. While it's boiling, grate in the bar of soap. As soon as it's melted turn the heat off. Pour the soda crystals into a jug and top it up with another 250ml water, then add it to the saucepan. Add 20 drops of your chosen essential oil. Keep mixing until it looks like risotto. Spoon it into a large, airtight glass jar.

Fresh-smelling fabric

To add a delicate fragrance to your clothes wash, take the lid off a nearly empty bottle of shower gel or hand wash and pop the bottle in the drum with a load of washing. It's best to check with your washing machine manufacturer beforehand to make sure you don't do any damage.

Lovely laundry basket

Sprinkle some flowery essential oil on to a paper towel, fold it up and pop it in the linen basket, so that even the dirty washing smells fresh as a daisy.

How to keep your clothes looking brand new for longer

A stitch in time can save your treasured clothes from the scrap heap. Sew buttons back on, patch elbows, turn up hems and polish shoes to give new life to old favourites.

Clean collars and cuffs

The collars and cuffs of shirts and blouses are magnets for dirt. You don't need expensive stain remover to get them pristine again; a paste made from washing powder will wash away the grime. Mix the powder with a little water, so that it forms a thick paste. Dab it on to the collar and cuffs and leave for 10 minutes. Then pop the shirt in the machine and wash as normal.

How to make a new shirt collar from the old one

For a just-like-new look, carefully unpick the collar from the shirt body using a seam ripper – these cost about £2.00 from a haberdashery department. Then unpick the stitching around the collar itself. Turn both sides inside out, and re-sew, then re-attach the fresh collar to the shirt.

How to remove chewing gum

Put the gummy garment in the freezer. Wait until the gum freezes, and then peel the wad off.

Socks appeal

If there's a hole in the toe of a woollen sock, but the rest of it is perfectly good, start unravelling and use the wool for something else. A stripy scarf a mile in length, for example.

Socks as sweatshirt cuffs

Raggedy cuffs on a favourite sweatshirt can be replaced with the tops of a pair of woollen socks. Cut off the old cuffs with sharp scissors. Snip off the ribbed tops from your socks using the discarded cuffs as a template. Carefully sew the snipped sock tops to the ends of the sleeves. Don't throw the shorter socks away; turn a little hem over on the top of each sock, machine-stitch and you've made a pair of trainer socks.

Bobbly jumper

Favourite jumper gone all bobbly? Restore to smoothness with a quick, gentle shave with a safety razor. Don't press too hard or the result will be bald patches and holes.

Waterproof an old umbrella

Over time umbrellas can loose their waterproofing. A quick way to restore it is with cheap hairspray. Spray the umbrella liberally, and head off into a rain shower.

How to stop trainers smelling

Banish nasty niffs with some cat litter. Spoon three tablespoons of cat litter into each offending trainer. Tuck in the tongues and laces. Leave overnight and the cat litter will absorb sweat, moisture and odour. In the morning, shake out the cat litter, and the trainers will smell as good as new.

Shiny shoes

These simple solutions will keep your footwear looking like new.

- The outsides of banana skins contain potassium, a key ingredient in commercial shoe polish. Rub the skins over the leather, and then buff with a soft, clean cloth

- Cheap hair conditioner works just as well as expensive shoe polish. Squeeze a little conditioner on to a clean cloth and rub over the shoes. Buff with a cloth to shine

- Sprinkle a tiny bit of cornflour on to stained suede. Leave if for 5–10 minutes and then brush it off. Reapply 2 or 3 times until the stain disappears.

A tip for ladder-free tights

The freezer is your friend. As soon as you buy new tights, pop them in for a few hours and it'll make the tights more resistant to laddering.

Three enterprising uses for old, clean tights

- Make a spice bag.

- Use them to strain lumpy paint.

- Fashion storage tubes for potatoes, onions or flower bulbs.

Beautiful bathrooms

Save money on everyday items and you can treat yourself to a home spa. Try some of the tips on pages 165–185.

Soapy savings

- Pop soap in the airing cupboard. It'll harden up in there and last longer – and if it's scented, your sheets will smell lovely.

- Hand wash can be pricey, but cheap cream bubble bath works just as well. Funnel some own brand bubble bath into a soap dispenser for bargain cleanliness.

- Save up old slivers of soap. Pop them, with a little olive oil, into a bowl and microwave until the slivers melt together. When the mixture's cooled slightly, squish it together and you'll have a new bar of soap.

Trapped toothpaste

It's amazing how much toothpaste can be left in a supposedly empty tube. Cut the tube in half with a small pair of scissors and dip your toothbrush into the hidden mint.

Toothsome bargains

Adult toothbrushes are expensive; cheaper children's toothbrushes will do just as well.

Making loo roll go further

If you squish the loo roll before putting it on the holder, it won't unravel like a party streamer, but instead turn over in economical sections.

Share the tub

An easy way to cut down on your water bills is to share the bath water. If you've got children, dip them in ascending height order, followed by you. And the last one in, if he's really grubby, can be the dog.

THE AVERAGE BRIT WASTES 50 LITRES OF WATER A DAY

Source: Waterwise, 2011

Don't waste bath water

After you've all had your bath, don't let the water out.

You can use it to:

- Flush the loo.
- Wash the car.
- Water the plants.

Flushed with success

Place an empty ice-cream tub in the toilet cistern. It will fill up with water, so that when you flush, it will use only three-quarters of the water in the tank, meaning you'll get one free flush in every four.

A fizzy loo cleaner

Cheap cola is a perfect loo cleaner. Pour a good glug into the toilet bowl. Leave for an hour or so then flush.

Or, sprinkle half a tub of bicarbonate of soda around the bowl and leave for 10 minutes. Then pour half a cup of vinegar over the soda. Sprinkle a couple of drops of eucalyptus oil around the toilet rim to kill any bothersome bacteria, and put the lid down. Leave for an hour, and then clean the bowl with a toilet brush.

A blocked loo

Chop the bottom off a plastic bottle with a kitchen knife. Leave the lid on. Holding it by the lid end push the bottle down into the blockage. Push it down as far as it will go, bring it out, push it down again and then bring it out really slowly. That should do the trick.

Unclogging the showerhead

Unscrew the showerhead, place it in a small bowl of vinegar and leave it to soak overnight. Give it a quick rinse in warm water, and then pop it back on the shower in the morning.

Cleaning a mouldy shower curtain

Before you embark on a rescue of your mildew-y shower curtains with bleach check the washing instructions on the curtains. All OK? Pop them in the machine on a cool wash. When the rinse cycle comes on, add two cups of bleach and let it do its work. At the end of the wash the mould should be gone.

SECRET OF THE SMALLEST ROOM

GOODNESS, MARY, FANCY USING THAT FOR YOUR LAVATORY!

BUT I WANT TO GET IT CLEAN

WHY NOT SPRINKLE IN A LITTLE **HARPIC**? LEAVE OVERNIGHT. THEN FLUSH. **HARPIC** REACHES RIGHT ROUND INTO THE S-BEND, LEAVES THE WHOLE BOWL SPOTLESS

HARPIC

Harpic Manufacturing Co. Ltd., Hull and London

Sort out your sink

Don't pour your hard-earned cash down drain. Gunge, smells and blocked plugholes can be dispelled by ordinary household products and a bit of elbow grease.

To sort out a blockage

- Crush up eggshells and pop them down the plughole. Their sharp edges will scour away old bits of food and gunk as they move through the U-bend.

- Cut a tennis ball in half. Put one half in the plughole, dome up, and give it a good pump.

- Gaffer tape will do the job, too. Put two pieces of gaffer tape over the overflow in the sink. Scrunch up a dishcloth and pump it up and down in the plughole ten times. The plug and the overflow are connected, so by covering the overflow the air will go where it's needed – down to the blockage – rather than whistling through the overflow.

Stinky sink? Our superscrimpers know what to do

- Pour half a cup of bicarbonate of soda down the plughole. Then pour one or two cups of heated white wine vinegar in after it. Leave for 10 minutes. Then flush it through with really hot water. The foam and froth will work its way down the pipes and flush out the trapped gunk and smelliness.

- Pour a generous scoop of soda crystals in the plughole and then pour on a whole kettle of boiling water.

A clean sink

Pop the plug into the sink and line the basin with kitchen paper to protect it from splashes. Put rubber gloves on and pour bleach around the basin. Leave for 30 minutes.

Remove the paper and wipe the basin with a sponge to bring out the shine.

Limescale taps

Pour vinegar into sandwich bags and put a sandwich bag over each tap, so that the limescale is submerged in the vinegar. Use duct tape to keep them in place and leave overnight. Remove the bags in the morning and wipe clean. But don't use on brass taps or any other coloured fixtures.

Fresh as a daisy

Room sprays can be expensive and can often smell overpoweringly artificial. Try these superscrimping ways for a breath of fresh air.

Air fresheners

- Strike a light, or rather, a match, in the vicinity of the bad odour and that will shift nasty niffs instantly.

- Wipe a cold radiator with a damp cloth sprinkled with essential oil. This will release a lovely scent as the radiator heats up.

- Pop a couple of scoops of bicarbonate of soda into a glass jar, and add a few drops of essential oil. Cut out a circle of lovely thrifted fabric – it needs to be bigger than the lid. Place it across the top of jar where the lid would go and hold in place with an elastic band.

Refresh dusty pot pourri

Dusty pot pourri is not enticing, so spruce it up by decanting it into a sandwich bag with a generous sprinkling of salt. Give the bag a good shake; the salt will knock off all the dust. Transfer the pot pourri to new bag, minus the salt and shake again. Put the now clean pot pourri into a bowl and revitalize the scent with a few drops of essential oil.

Carpet freshener

Smelly carpet? Get out the bicarbonate of soda. Sprinkle it liberally over the offending areas, leave it for about 15 minutes and then hoover it up.

Or, generously spray perfume on to cotton wool. Put the cotton wool in the bag of your vacuum cleaner. As you vacuum the airflow will give a lovely waft of scent.

MAKE A HOUSE A HOME

THE AVERAGE BRIT SPENDS £158,000 ON HOME DECORATING AND REFURBISHMENT OVER A LIFETIME.

Source: Isme.com, 2013

Divine décor

With a little art know-how, some cut-price creativity and a knack for making more from other people's cast-offs, you can turn trash into treasure and a humble house into a cosy home that's full of original touches. And share the wealth by turning these crafty ideas into hand-made gifts.

Decorative pots for indoor plants

Give old tin cans and metal containers a make-over. Measure round the can and its height. Cut out a piece of sticky-backed plastic to the can's dimensions and carefully smooth it on. You can also use wallpaper or wrapping paper – stick these down with craft glue. Or, if fabric is your decorative choice, use good-quality fabric glue. Add compost and a pert peony.

> Get scissor happy by folding some recycled tin foil until it's several layers thick. Use blunt scissors to cut through the layers to re-sharpen the blades.

Paper flowers

Old magazines and discarded wrapping paper can be folded and cut into perky table decorations. Fold the paper in half and then in half again. Cut into a petal shape then snip off the corner fold. For filigree flowers cut small holes in the petal shapes. Make lots more petals then layer lots of them together and thread them on to sticks through the central holes. Use sticky tape to keep the blooms steady.

Decorative bottles

Make good use of your empties by turning humble glass bottles into stylish vases. Wash the glass bottles thoroughly. Hold the bottle over some newspaper and spray with spray paint in the colour of your choice, in a very well ventilated area. Two or three light coats of paint will be enough for a drip-free finish. Let the paint dry and then style with a single bright bloom in the neck of each bottle.

A jewellery frame

An old picture frame acquired from a charity shop, car boot sale
or the corner of the attic can be made into a jewellery display board.
Take the back off the frame, (and the glass front if there is one) and
glue cork wall tiles on to the backing. Pop it back into the frame.
Push brightly coloured pins into the cork tiles and dangle your
jewellery from them, in tangle free profusion.

A ribbon light pull

Replace a dingy bathroom light pull with this prettier version.

You will need:
a doubled-over length of wide ribbon
string
something heavy for the weight like a big key or a spoon

Switch off the lighting circuit and detach the light pull. Thread the
string under the fold of the ribbon, leaving a little hanging out of
the end; this will be tied to the old light pull on the ceiling. Sew
along the long edges of the ribbon, folding over the ends to make
a neat edge. Stitch your weight to the ribbon securely - you don't
want it to come off when the light is turned on and off. Check the
circuit is still switched off and attach the string to the light fitting.

A corking coat hook

Drill three evenly spaced holes along a length of wood. Screw in
three dowel screws (these are double-headed screws) and screw
three corks on to each screw to act as hooks.

Cheeky chalk boards

You can transform practically any surface in your house into a chalkboard using blackboard paint, which you can buy in hardware shops (see Blackboard plant pots, page xxx).

- A battered old wooden table is just the thing for a lick of blackboard paint. Sand down the top with sand paper, working against the grain. Wipe clean and apply two coats of blackboard paint. Perfect for a creative dinnertime.

- You could make a blackboard tray. Clean and sand an old wooden tray, a leftover piece of wood, or a stray cupboard door. Paint with blackboard paint. If the wood is very porous you may have to apply a couple of coats. Leave to dry. You can chalk up the day's specials on the tray, and serve dinner on it, too.

A Christmas garland

A festive Christmas garland festooning the stairs is beautiful, but extravagant ones can be costly. Instead, buy the cheapest one you can and then wind lots of greenery and berries from your garden through it. It looks lovely and is fun to make.

A fabric garland

It's easy to make this shabby-chic garland from old fabric. Get a bundle of brightly coloured material and cut it into strips and then tie the strips to string or twine. Hang the garlands in festive swoops.

A swish paper pom-pom

Need to posh up a party venue, but short of pence? These elegant paper pom-poms cost pennies to make, but look very chic.

Layer ten sheets of tissue paper, one on top of the other. Fold them

in a concertina effect and tie a piece of wire around the middle. Cut the ends of the tissue paper folds to petal-shaped points. Open out the ends, and start slowly pulling up the layers, fluffing out the paper as you go.

Thread a ribbon through the wire to hang the pom-pom from the ceiling. For an even more extravagant decoration, put one finished pom-pom on top of another.

Candlelit comfort

Creative lighting can make all the difference to the feel of a room. Give your home a warm glow with these crafty candles.

Teacup candles

Teacup candles make lovely gifts, and they can be made for practically nothing. Charity shops are a great place to find cups and saucers, and you can use the stubs of old candles to make a new one.

You will need:
candle stubs
a piece of string or parcel twine
a teacup and saucer

a metal jug
sticky tape

Put the candle stubs in a heatproof container and stand it in a pan of hot water to melt the wax.

Dip the end of the string in the melting wax and stick it to the

bottom of the teacup. Stick some sticky tape across the top of the cup, and secure the string to it so that the string is verticle in the centre of the cup.

As soon as the wax has melted, remove the container from the pan. Be really, really careful as you take the jug off the heat. Slowly pour the wax into the teacup and set it aside to cool down and set. Whip off the sticky tape before lighting the candle.

· ·

Recycled scented candles

Often when scented candles burn away you're left with a hollow shell; these can be melted and made into a new candle.

You will need:
wax shells of burnt candles
a glass jar
a piece of string or parcel twine

cardboard

Break up the wax shells and put them in a little glass jar. Put the jar on top of the radiator and leave it to melt.

Cut a strip of cardboard that's wider than your glass jar. Make a hole in the middle of the cardboard and thread the twine through the hole. Tie a knot in one end of the twine to stop it slipping through the card and balance the card over the jar, letting the other end of the twine dangle to the bottom of the wax. Put the glass jar in a bowl of cold water until the wax sets, then cut the twine to a nice wick size.

A designer candle

Charity shops and car boot sales are great places to find retro glass bowls. Add candles to the mix and you'll be bowled over by how classy it looks.

You will need:
100g paraffin wax
candle stubs
essential oil
a fancy glass bowl
4 tealights

an old teapot or measuring jug

> Freeze candles and tealights to make them last longer. The coldness hardens the wax so it burns for longer.

Melt all the wax together in a bowl placed over a simmering saucepan of water. Shake in about 20 drops of your favourite essential oil. Once melted, decant the wax into an old teapot or measuring jug and pour a layer of wax into the bowl.

Arrange the tealights in the wax layer and then pour the rest of the wax into the bowl so that it covers the tealights, but not their wicks. *Voilà* — a stylish candle designed by you!

Hanging tealights

These look gorgeous hanging from a tree or along the clothesline. Make lots of them for a summer party.

You will need:
a clean jam jar
a long length of garden wire
a tealight

Wrap the garden wire around the top
of the jar twice Twist the short
end of wire around the long end
a few times to secure it. Feed
the long end of the wire back
through the loop you've
just made and round to
the other side of the jar.
Pull up the wire to make
a handle, and twist the
end around the end of the
handle to hold it all in place. Drop in a
tealight and hang from a low branch in
the garden.

DON'T THROW AWAY YOUR CANDLE STUBS, YOU COULD

Melt them down to
make more candles
(see pages 111–113).

Un-stick a reluctant
car window (see
page 237).

Lubricate an old
saw (see page 193).

Tin-can lantern

These easy-to-make lanterns will give you and your home a warm glow.

Thoroughly scrub the label off the tin, then fill it with water and put it in the freezer. Once the water has frozen solid, take it out of the freezer and draw a design of your choice on the tin. Rest it on a folded towel to protect your work surface.

Your frozen tin can now bear the brunt of a hammering so, with a nail and hammer, punch holes around the outline of your design. Let the ice thaw and then pop a candle or a tealight inside.

Prudently practical

Practical doesn't have to be plain, here are some pretty, tidy ways to save the pennies.

A pretty storage tub

Glitz up an old plastic tub with some leftover wrapping paper. Measure the dimensions of the tub. Mark those measurements on to the wrong side of the wrapping paper and cut it out. Cover the back of the paper with glue and carefully smooth it against the plastic.

Cereal storage

Those giant boxes of breakfast cornflakes are just the right size to store magazines. With a sharp craft knife or scissors cut off the opening flaps of the packet. On one of the thin sides of the box, measure 10cms up from the bottom and pencil in a straight line across. On the broad sides of the box draw a diagonal line from the end of the short pencil line to the opposite corner of the packet. Following the pencilled guide lines, cut away the cardboard. Now carefully take the box apart and cover with wallpaper, strong brown paper or fabric. Reassemble the box and glue it back together.

● ●

Découpage tray

Add a playful, original look to a past-its-best tray with some dashing decoupage.

You will need:
a metal tray
white emulsion paint
colourful paper – scraps from magazines, old wallpaper, wrapping paper, etc.
varnish

sandpaper
glue

Remove any rust from the tray with sandpaper, then paint it with a coat of white paint. Cut out a variety of patterns and shapes from your stash of decorative paper. Arrange the paper pieces in pleasing patterns and glue them on to the tray. Cover with a coat of varnish to give a glossy finish and protect your design from wear and tear. Make sure the varnish is dry before serving tea on your treasure-from-trash tray.

A scrap of fabric

Even oddments of fabric can be transformed into something useful and unusual. Here are some magic ideas to make the most of your material.

A cheap way of getting cut-price craft items is to join the charity scrap-stores scheme. You pay a small annual membership fee and then you can purchase donated crafty items for much less than high-street prices. Check out www.scrapstoresuk.org for details.

Denim draught excluder

Stop the wind whistling in under the door with this quirky denim draught excluder. Cut the leg off an old pair of jeans. Turn it inside out and tidy up the raggedy edge by machine-stitching a small hem along the cut end. Stuff with old towels or sheets then screw up each end like a Christmas cracker. Secure with elastic bands then hide these with ribbons tied into big bows.

A laptop cover

Keep your laptop free from scratches with this vintage-style cover. A salvaged charity-shop curtain is perfect for the cover and you can buy the felt from craft shops and haberdashers.

You will need:

2 rectangles of felt, at least 1cm bigger all round than your laptop

2 rectangles of fabric, cut bigger than your scraps of felt

fabric glue
scissors
needle
thread

Take one piece of fabric, turn the two longs sides over about 1cm, wrong sides together, and glue down. Fold the shorter sides in the same way. Fold in the corners and glue them down, too. Glue a felt rectangle on to the fabric to cover up all the rough edges. Do exactly the same thing with the other pieces of fabric and felt. Place the two fabric pieces together, felt sides touching, and hand sew around three sides with zigzag or blanket stitch. You can now slide the computer into its funky cover.

Perfect placemat

Leftover curtain material is perfect for this project. You'll need two pieces of fabric for each placemat. Cut a template from old newspaper to the size you want your placemat to be. Pin it to the fabric, or trace the outline with tailor's chalk (this brushes off easily) and cut the fabric out with sharp scissors. Pin the right sides of the fabric together. Machine-stitch around three of the sides, about 1.5cm in from the edge. Remove the pins and turn the placemat the right way out. Use a knitting needle to poke out the corners. Fold in the fourth edge and machine-stitch in place.

Handy heat packs

Heat packs are perfect for soothing tired and achy muscles. Make sure you don't use instant or quick-cook rice or the pack will get too hot. Remember to check the temperature of the pack before you apply it to your skin.

- Fold an old napkin in half and machine-stitch around the sides, leaving a small gap. Use a funnel to pour enough rice through the gap so that the pack is full but still flexible. Hand-stitch the gap and then sprinkle on a few drops of soothing lavender oil. Heat in the microwave for no longer than a minute.

- Ah, another odd sock. Half fill it with rice. Sew up the top of the sock, and pop it in the microwave for 2 minutes, and hey presto, you've made a snugly heat pack to keep you warm throughout the winter.

A computer wrist rest

Charity shops shelves are often full of lovely old-fashioned doilies. Give them a modern makeover and transform them into wrist rests, a dainty solution to the problems of RSI.

You will need:

a round doily (not one that's made of lace or the rice will fall out)
rice
sewing machine or a needle and thread
kitchen funnel

Fold the doily in half to make a semicircle. Stitch nearly all the way round the curved edge, but leave a small gap. Pop a kitchen funnel into the gap and pour in some rice. Fill the doily until it's reasonably firm, and hand-stitch the gap.

A lavender bag

Fold a printed hanky by a third. Then fold it in half. Sew 2 of the sides. Sprinkle dried lavender on to a piece of wadding and fold it over so that the lavender doesn't escape. (Lacking wadding? Use old tights instead.) Pop the wadding into the hanky bag, wrap a pretty piece of ribbon around the bag and tie it in a bow.

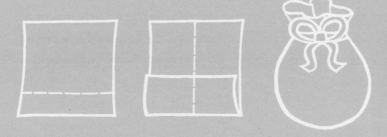

A flowery moth repellent

Moths love to munch on woollies. But here's a cheap way to keep them at bay. Cut out two squares of cotton fabric. Machine-stitch three of the sides, wrong sides together. Stuff the fabric bag with some dried flowers, and lavender, which moths despise – add a few drops of lavender oil to boost the effect. Machine-stitch the final side. Trim the edges of the bag with pinking shears for a pretty zigzag look. Add a ribbon loop and a decorative bow, and hang it in your wardrobe. Your clothes will smell of summer meadows while the moths will be disgusted.

A scented heart on a ribbon

These scented hearts look and smell sweet.

You will need:
charming old fabric
an old pillow
essential oil
ribbon
pinking shears

Cut out two heart shapes from your pretty fabric with the pinking shears, as this gives the edge a lovely zigzag finish. Sew up the heart, but leave a gap at the heart's pointed end. Pluck out some stuffing from the old pillow (it's a good idea to save old pillows for a cheap source of stuffing) and stuff it into the fabric heart. Drop a little scented oil on to the stuffing and sew up the gap. Sew the ribbon in a loop to the top of the heart and hang from the mantelpiece or a doorknob.

A drawstring laundry bag

Transform an old tablecloth into a lovely laundry bag.

You will need:

a tablecloth

optional: scraps of fabric to appliqué on to the bag

2 long lengths of ribbon

newspaper

scissors

pins

sewing machine or needle and thread

a big safety pin

Decide how big you want your bag to be and make a newspaper template, remembering to add in an extra 5cm for a large hem at the top and 2cm for the side seams.

Fold the tablecloth in half and pin the bottom of the template along the fold. Cut around it with sharp scissors. If you want to appliqué a design or a name on to the bag, now's the time to do it. Cut out shapes or letters from the scraps of fabric and sew them on to the right side of the bag.

With right sides together, sew up the sides of the bag. Turn a hem over on the top edges, on the wrong side, and machine-stitch two rows along the top edge, about 2cm apart; this is where the drawstring is going to go. Nip a little hole in the stitching at each side to make little gaps at each end of the channel you've just sewn. Attach a safety pin to one length of ribbon and thread it between the rows of stitching, pulling it all the way through and out where it went in. Attach the safety pin to the other length of ribbon, and push it through the gap in the opposite direction from the first ribbon. Load up with laundry and then pull your drawstring together so nothing escapes.

Classy cushion covers

- T-shirts with bright prints or bold mottos make great cushion covers. Buy stuffing from the craft shop, or use the innards of an old pillow. Turn the T-shirt inside out. Cut straight across below the sleeves. Stitch up the sides, but leave a gap so you can fill it with the stuffing. Turn the T-shirt the right way round and get stuffing. Stitch the gap closed.

- Sew together a few pieces of scrap fabric and re-cover old cushions with a gorgeous patchwork design.

Beanbags

Old curtain material is perfect for beanbags. Stock up on polystyrene beads from the craft shop, or use the polystyrene that comes as packaging in parcels. If your sewing is a little rickety, the bin bag will stop the beads from escaping and creating a polystyrene snow blizzard in the front room

You will need:

polystyrene beads
a large piece of curtain fabric
a bin bag

scissors
sewing machine or a needle and thread

Fold the curtain fabric in half, short edges and right sides together, and stitch two of the three loose sides. Turn the fabric the right way round. Put the polystyrene beads in a bin liner, and tie securely. Put the bin liner inside the curtains, and stitch the last side closed.

Practical HOME MONEY MAKER

1'3

EDITOR : F. J. CAMM

NOVEMBER 195

Contents

MAKING DRESS JEWELLERY; SIGNWRITING; VENEERED WOODWORK FOR THE CHRISTMAS TRADE; LEATHER WORKING; MAKING TOYS AND NOVELTIES; LOOSE COVERS FOR PROFIT; MUSHROOMS—A PAYING SIDELINE

Upcycled elegance

With a little imagination you can upcycle your shabby old furniture. A lick of leftover paint, a decorative flourish or two and your trash becomes vintage-inspired treasure. Head for charity shops, recycling centres and car boot sales to search out bargains, and don't be afraid to haggle.

IN THE UK, WE SPEND £650 A YEAR ON NEW FURNITURE.

Source: www.bfm.org.uk

Haggling

If you're sourcing old furniture from shops and markets, don't be afraid to quibble on the price. Old furniture is only as valuable as the price you're willing to pay for it. Good luck!

- Do a bit of research beforehand. Know how much you would have to pay elsewhere, and then start negotiating.

- Always start with a low offer, and don't blurt out your maximum budget at the beginning.

- Look for flaws; a small imperfection can mean big savings.

- And if something has already been reduced, chances are you'll be able to get it even cheaper, as it's obviously not a bestseller.

A crash course in reupholstering a dining chair

This works really well for chairs with a solid base. Webbing or canvas bases would need to be replaced. Always wear a mask.

Whip off the old fabric and remove the stuffing and any horsehair, which is itchy and scratchy to sit on. Tease out any tacks with pliers.

Measure the seat, and cut the foam to fit its dimensions. Use a bread knife to cut the foam with downward strokes. Glue the foam to the chair. Put some wadding on top of the foam for extra comfiness.

Drape your new fabric over the new seat. Holding it in place, put in four staples with a staple gun, one for each corner of the seat, to stop it shifting round. Pull the fabric taut and staple all the way round the chair. Fold the front corners in neatly and staple in place. Trim any excess.

Cover any visible staples by sticking on scraps of trimming with a glue gun.

Painting old wooden furniture

Sand the wood in the direction of the grain using medium-grade sandpaper, just roughing it up a little. The rough surface will help the paint adhere. You can use whatever paint you have – from emulsion to gloss. Don't overload the brush. Brush on an even coat, then leave to dry.

- To give a distressed, antique look to the fresh paintwork, gently rub down sections with sandpaper. Sand the areas you'd expect to find wear and tear.

- For a fancy flourish, dab a kitchen sponge in the lid of a paint tin in a different colour to your base coat. Blot the excess paint on some newspaper, and then lightly rest the sponge against the paintwork. Use clear varnish to seal and protect the paint.

- Cut out designs from wallpaper for stencils. Place the stencil on the surface you want to decorate. Use a sponge to dab the paint on to the surface, through the stencil. Make sure you don't overlaod the sponge or the paint will leak.

Transform a glass-topped coffee table

A really simple way to give a glass-topped table a new lease of life is to lift out the glass panel and give the base a lick of paint. Then paste wallpaper or striking fabric on to the surface of the table underneath where the glass usually sits. Lower the glass top back into place and you have a designer table that looks brand new.

Revamp an old lamp

An old-fashioned lamp can be given an up-to-the-minute look with a new-from-old shade. Carefully remove the old, shabby trimmings from the lamp. Measure round the shade and cut some scrap fabric to the shade's measurements. Spray adhesive spray to the original lampshade and carefully smooth on the new fabric. Let it dry. Spread a thin line of fabric glue along the edge of the fabric and finish the lamp with a row of pom-pom trimming.

Dog-bed suitcase

A battered old suitcase can easily become a dandy dog's bed. Cut off the lid and discard. Paint the bottom of the suitcase in dashing coats of emulsion. Leave to dry. Paint on a coat of varnish. Cover an old bed pillow in some poochy fabric and pop it into the suitcase. Add dog.

Gift-wrap the superscrimping way

Wrapping paper and gift bags can cost as much as the present you're giving. Follow these tips for stylish presents for half the price.

Reliable wrapping

- To make wrapping paper as good as new simply iron out the creases. The heat from the iron will loosen any lingering pieces of sticky tape, which can then be peeled off.

- Pages from colour supplements and glossy magazines can make very original wrapping paper. Add salvaged bows and ribbons for a dash of cheap chic.

- A roll of brown paper, some saved ribbon and a sparkly piece of broken junk jewellery make for cheap but unique gift-wrapping.

Christmas gift tags

Turning old Christmas Cards into brand new gift tags is a crafty way to save money. Cut a Christmassy image from the front of a card, punch a hole at the top and thread string or ribbon through the hole so that it can be attached to the gift.

Customized cards

Add a personal touch to cards by making your own, each with their own unique message. Cut out brightly coloured letters from magazines and newspapers and glue them on to some folded card. Be as cheeky or as sincere as you like.

Top toys

Double the fun with these home-made toys by getting the kids involved with the creative process. They'll have the time of their lives making them, and end up with something that's entirely special to them.

A sock-monster soft toy

Making a sock monster is a chance to go a bit wild with your sewing skills. It's also a great way to use up crafty odds and ends. There's no need to buy expensive craft stuffing, the innards of an old pillow work just as well.

Note: This toy is not suitable for children under three years of age

You will need:
a colourful sock
buttons
pom-poms
snippets of felt
feathers
stuffing

needle and thread

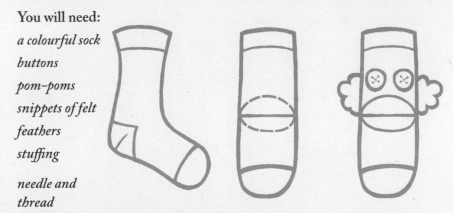

Turn the sock inside out and sew a running stitch around the heel to make the mouth shape. Turn the sock right way round, and start stuffing the body. Sew the bottom edge of the monster to stop the stuffing spilling out. Sew on buttons for eyes, and then get busy with the other bits and bobs. Add a tail feather, pom-pom ears, fierce white felt teeth or whatever takes your fancy.

Puppet bath toy

Fold an old hand-towel in half. Put your hand palm-down on the towel, with your wrist on the fold, keeping your three middle fingers together, but spreading out the thumb and little finger – these will be the puppet's arms. Draw around your hand with a permanent marker.

Cut out the puppet shape, adding 2cm all the way round for the seam, then snip along the fold so you have a back and a front.

Using washable felt, add some creature features and hand-sew them on securely. With right sides facing, stitch the puppet together. If you're going for a pointy ear look, cut them out and pop them point down between the layers of towel before sewing together. Turn the puppet right side out and run the water for a fun-filled bathtime.

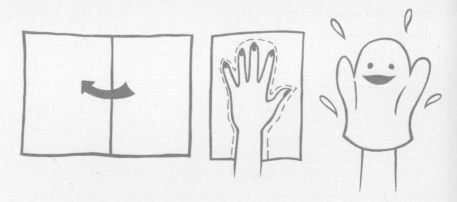

Homemade play dough

This dough is easy to make, and it's completely safe if your child eats it as well as plays with it.

You will need:
2 cups of flour
1 cup of salt
1 tbsp oil
a few drops of food colouring

Mix the ingredients together in a big bowl until they form a dough. Give it a good knead and it's ready for playtime.

Crayons

When crayons have worn down to a stub and are hard to hold, don't throw them away. Instead pop the crayon stubs into a cake case, on a foil-covered baking tray. Heat them in the oven at 200°C/400°F/ gas mark 6 for 10 minutes. As soon as they've cooled down, take the melded crayon out of the cake case, and start drawing with your new multi-coloured crayon.

FRUGAL FASHION

One million tonnes of unwanted clothes are thrown out in the UK each year.

Source: www.defra.gov.uk, 2011

With a little nifty needlework, a bit of imaginative thinking and a supply of sequins, buttons and bows your old clothes can be remade into something new and fabulous. Change hemlines, swap sleeves and replace white plastic buttons with cool hand-covered ones – stitch rather than ditch is the superscrimper's frugal fashion motto.

Here are a few handy tips:

- Charity shops are a brilliant place to track down cheap chic, vintage curtain fabric and bold buttons for your button jar.

- Look in the window first – often the best things are on display.

- Most people donate at the weekends, so visit early in the week when all the good stuff will have just been put out.

- Have a good old rummage; you never know what treasure is lurking at the back of a shelf or squashed on a rail.

- Pick your postcode. Up-market areas will have up-market fashion labels.

- Snap up classics – cashmere, tweed and silk never go out of fashion.

Creative customizing

These ideas involve very few sewing skills and most can be made with bits and bobs you already have in your house. Have fun designing your own fashion collection.

Bleached T-shirt

It's easy to jazz up an old T-shirt with cheap toilet bleach. Place a piece of cardboard or a magazine inside the T-shirt to stop the bleach from seeping through to the other side. Chalk your design on to the front. Pour the bleach into a cup and paint along the chalk lines using an old paintbrush. The colour will fade quickly so once you get the colour you want, pop it straight into the wash. It's best to wear old clothes when doing this, and be careful not to get bleach on your skin.

Make a vest from a T-shirt

A funky little vest is just the thing for the summer weather, but there's no need to buy new when old will do . Cut the sleeves off a T-shirt then cut a big scoop from the front of the neck to make a vest shape. Where you've cut along the seams, sew a stitch or two with a needle and thread to stop things unravelling, and you're good to go.

Buttoned up

Dandify an old shirt or cardigan with some lovely handmade buttons. Snip off the old buttons and add them to your button jar. To replace them you'll need some shank buttons – these are the ones with the loop at the back – and some pretty fabric. Cut rough 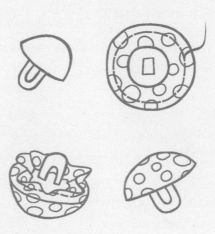 and ready circles out of the fabric – these should be twice the circumference of the button head. Hand sew a line of running stitch around the edge of the fabric circle. Leaving the needle and thread attached to the fabric, put the fabric over the button and pull the thread so that the fabric tightens around the button. Play around with the fabric so that it looks nice and smooth on the front, and neat on the back. Secure with a few stitches at the back. Knot the thread, and snip it off. Sew your new-look buttons on to your shirt or cardie.

Pillow-case apparel

You can pick up pillowcases for pennies from charity shops and car boot sales. And it's easy to transform them into a cool summer top.

Fold the pillowcase in half, lengthways. Chalk a semicircle scoop for the armholes, and another for the neck. Cut round the scoops and shake out the pillowcase. *Et voila*: a cute summer top.

To stop the fabric fraying, sew on some bias binding in a matching or contrasting colour. This last tip can be seen as a decorative extra; it will bump up the price of your cut-price top, but it's pretty and practical, too.

A top made from two scarves

This sophisticated summer top couldn't be easier to make. Sew two scarves, right sides together, across the top edges, leaving a gap for your head. Sew down the sides, right sides together, leaving gaps for you arms. Turn the right way out. Gather the fabric at the shoulders with a clip-on earring. Pull over your head and wear with a belt to cinch in the waist.

Sequins and beads

Snip sequins and beads from clothes you don't wear any more and sew them on to something else to give it a shiny new identity. Take an everyday cardigan to out-on-the-town evening wear by sewing on beads or sequins in clusters of three.

New shirts from old

Unpick the sleeves and pockets from two shirts. Swap over the sleeves and pockets, pin and machine-stitch them in place and you have two new looks from two tired shirts.

A floaty dress

Look a million pounds on a shoestring budget, with virtually no effort. Buy a pleated granny skirt with an elasticated waist – the charity shops are full of them. Hoick it up over your boobs and add a skinny belt to accentuate your curves.

How to make shorts from jeans

Lay out the jeans flat. Think about how short you want them to be and add about 5cm to that measurement to allow for a double turn-up. Cut both legs at the same time to ensure they're the same length, pull them on and turn up the hem once, and then again.

To get a fashionably faded look, a bit of distressing puts a vintage twist on your new shorts. File away at the fabric for a few minutes with a nail file. If you want to rip it, get great results with the cheese grater. Gently pull it across the fabric for an aged denim look.

Legwarmers

Shrink a woollen jumper in a hot wash and snip off the arms
for instant leg warmers.

Revamp an old jumper

Jazz up an old jersey by upcycling it into a dress in a matter
of minutes. First cut straight across the torso of the jumper just
underneath the armholes. Measure a piece of fabric that's twice the
width of the jumper, with a bit extra for the seams. Cut the fabric
out. Fold the fabric, right sides together, and machine-stitch the
short sides together to make a tube. Sew the tube to the cut-up
jumper, right sides together to cover up the raw edges. Hey presto,
a new frock!

How to make a wristband from an odd sock

There's always a lonesome odd sock lying in the sock drawer. Instead of throwing it out, upcycle it into a wristband. Cut the sock above the heel. Fold the cut edge under and machine-stitch to stop it fraying.

Old top, new fingerless gloves

Cut the sleeves off an old top. Put your hand in and push your fingers out the end to work out where your thumb should go. Cut a small hole for your thumb. Stitch a hem on the top and bottom edges of the gloves so they don't fray, and do the same around the thumbholes. Customize your creations with some cute buttons.

Bags of opportunity

You can never have too many bags, and these designs are so simple to make, you can update your look every season.

Jean Genius bag

Cut the legs off a pair of old jeans and then cut off the front (the zip, etc.) so you're left with a long rectangle of denim.

Fold it in half, short sides together, with the right sides facing each other. Pin along the sides and the bottom of your bag shape, and machine-stitch in place.

Use the legs for handles. Cut two long strips of denim (to whatever length you'd like your handles). With an iron, press a little hem all the way round one strip and then do the same on the other one. Sew one strip to the other, wrong sides together. Turn the bag inside out. Pin the handle to the inside of the bag and sew it on. Turn the jean genius bag the right way out.

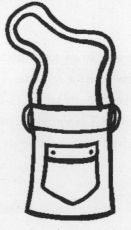

OLD JEANS ARE EXTREMELY VERSATILE. YOU CAN ALSO:

Turn your jeans into vintage-style shorts (see page 143)

Make cute bows to sew on just about anything (see page 150)

Create a draught excluder (see page 118)

Jolly up a straw beach bag

Make your straw tote stand out from the crowd with the addition of a few smart accessories. Glue a broken necklace to the side and use an old spotty scarf as a lining, by hand-sewing it to the inside of the bag. Tie a brightly patterned scarf to the bag's handle for a touch of summer swagger.

Belts, hats, shoes and bows

Accessorize, accessorize, accessorize.

Winning ways with a hat

Give an old floppy hat a film-star makeover. Think Audrey Hepburn, but with more dash than cash.

- Wrap a scarf around the hat and tie it in a knot or a bow. Pop a string of beads over the crown. The beads will look lovely and will also stop the hat blowing away on a windy day.

- Find two ribbons in contrasting colours, one thinner than the other. Glue the thinner ribbon to the wider one, wait until they're dry and then tie them around the hat and secure in a knot or bow.

Bedazzle a belt

Stick-on diamanté and jewels are an easy way to jazz up a charity shop belt. Use good-quality craft glue or a glue gun. Handbags, shoes and tops can all be brightened up with some bling.

A scarf belt

Cut a headscarf straight down the middle almost to the end. Flip one half over and fold it over the other half, so you have one long

piece of fabric that is double-sided. Neatly sew along the middle. Fold over the edges and sew them, so that they're nice and neat. Tie around your waist like a sash and sashay forth.

Feathers for flappers

Get a 1920s look with a stiff hairband and a couple of feathers. Pick a big bold feather, spread glue down its centre stem and carefully stick it on to one side of the hair band. Then take another feather, in a contrasting shape and colour, and glue that on top of the first feather. Wait until the glue is entirely dry. Place in your hair, and think about taking Charleston lessons.

Feathered buttonholes

Instead of flower buttonholes, make a feathered favour. Assemble different coloured feathers; play around with colour combinations until you find the one you like best. Bind your chosen arrangement with sticky tape and pin it to your suit or blouse.

Fabric bows

A sweet fabric bow is an appealing addition to jeans, tops and bags. And they're very simple to make. Take a strip of fabric and fold it in half lengthways. Sew along the open sides. Fold the ends of the fabric into the middle, pinch the centre of the fabric to make a bow shape, and sew securely with a few stitches.

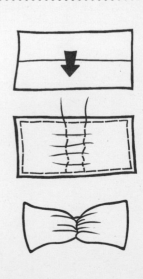

Swishing

Have a go at swishing – it's the perfect solution to a free frock. Photograph your unworn clothes and upload the images on to sites such as www.swishing.co.uk. The sites then rate them, and give you virtual money credits to be used against any items on the website. With a minimum swap-fee of a thrifty 50p it's a great way to update your entire wardrobe.

Host your own free shopping spree by inviting your friends over, making sure everyone brings at least one quality item. Allow half an hour of browsing, then swap away.

Check out these websites for advice on hosting your own swap parties along with info on nationwide swishing events:

www.swishing.co.uk

www.swishing.com

www.swishingparties.com

CUSTOMIZED SHOES

Bored with your pumps? Tired with your trainers? Here are some clever ways to make you fall in love with your feet.

You could:

- Pretty-up plain pumps or court shoes by painting the toe area in a contrasting colour – make sure you use waterproof paint.

- Swap the laces with ribbons, glue on gems, studs or rosebuds.

- Paint on glittery nail polish to add shimmery sparkle.

- Go for go-faster stripes fashioned from fabric: grab some bold, bright fabric and a pair of old trainers. Cut out a tongue-shaped piece of fabric. Glue down the straight edge to make it nice and neat. Slick some glue over the trainer tongue, and cover with your new fabric, folding over the edges and gluing for a neat finish.

- Now for the stripes: cut out a 3cm-wide strip of fabric. Fold the fabric in on itself on both sides, lengthwise, and glue together. Cut them into smaller strips and glue them to the trainers wherever you think they look the coolest.

Fancy flip-flops

Cheap flip-flops are easy to come by, but they can look a little lacklustre, so jazz them up with handmade rosettes. Take a length of ribbon, make a fold and put a stitch in with needle and thread. Make another fold and put another stitch in. Keep folding and stitching all the way round. Sew a bright button on to the middle of each rosette to hide your stitches and then glue the rosettes to the middle of your flip-flops.

Jazzy jewellery

With a little bit of glue, and a big dash of imagination you can transform junk to jewellery, adding up to some precious savings. Good as gold.

Funky feather diamanté earrings

There's no need to buy glittery diamanté jewels for these earrings, just use the ones that have fallen off your top.

You will need:
different coloured feathers
wire
fishhook earrings
diamanté jewels

glue

Make two small bundles of feathers by gluing along their stems. Leave them to dry. Wrap wire around the stems and twist a little loop in the wire to attach it to each earring. Hook the earring to the wire. Finish off with some bling by gluing the diamanté jewels on to the feathers.

Lovely lacy earrings

Cut dainty lace circles or flowers from old curtains. To make them less floppy, mix PVA glue and water in equal parts and dip the lace

in the solution. Allow to dry. With flat-nose pliers insert a jump
ring into the lace. And then attach fishhook earrings.

Bold button earrings

Raid the button jar for two beguiling buttons. Snip the backs off
with pliers (if they have them) and glue earring posts – you can buy
these from craft shops – to the back of the buttons. Leave to dry.

Ravishing ribbon earrings

Hoop earrings can be jazzed up with just a twist and a twirl of
ribbon. Glue a brightly coloured piece of ribbon to the earrings and
wrap it tightly over and over
around the hoop. When you
get to the end of the earring,
glue down the ribbon, and
leave it to dry. Cut off any
excess ribbon. It's so easy to
do that you change ribbon
colour as often as you
change outfits.

Natty neon necklace

Bored with a bland old necklace? Give it bold makeover. Spray it
any shade you like, but neon brights add a dramatic pop of colour.
Lay the necklace on newspaper in a very well-ventilated space and
spray evenly all over. Let the paint dry then add a second coat.
Finish with two coats of clear gloss spray for a high-shine look.

Pretty paper bead necklace

Pep up an old chain with some charming paper beads. Gather up brightly coloured wrapping paper, a pencil, scissors and glue. Cut the paper into strips. Glue along the short edge of a strip of paper on the patterned side and then wrap the paper over and over around the pencil. Keep wrapping and when you've finished rolling, dab a bit of glue on to the end of the paper so that the bead doesn't unravel. Pull it off the pencil straightaway so it doesn't get stuck. Make more beads and then thread them on to the chain.

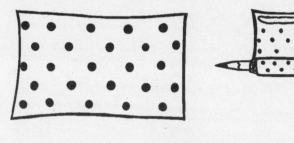

Delightful daisy necklace

Don't stop at daisies; use the clay to create a garden of jewellery flowers, a rain cloud and a rainbow, or anything else that comes to mind. Read the manufacture's instructions before getting started wiht the modelling clay for this project.

You will need:

yellow modelling clay
white modelling clay

a necklace chain

2 jump rings

flat-nosed pliers

a cocktail stick or pin

Roll a small ball of yellow clay and flatten it to make the flower's centre. Make a circle of white petals from the white clay and press them on to the yellow circle.

Use a cocktail stick or pin to punch holes in two of the petals; this is where you'll attach the chain. Bake the clay flower and leave to harden. Pop jump rings in the holes using the flat-nosed pliers and thread the chain on to the jump rings.

Memory wire bracelet

You can buy memory wire from bead shops and craft suppliers. It's brilliant for making jewellery as it holds its shape.

Cut a length of wire that can wrap around your wrist with a little room to spare. Make a loop at one end of the wire using round-nosed pliers – this will stop the beads from falling off. Thread on a bold, bright arrangement of beads. Make another loop with the pliers at the other end of the bracelet and attach a charm for extra pizzazz.

Friendship bracelets

You need strands of ribbon to make this plaited bracelet – multiples of three work best. (You could use the free ribbon that comes as a hanging loop in the shoulders of your clothes, or buy some in your local haberdashery.)

Bundle the ribbons together and tie a knot 5cm from the end. Plait it all the way to the bottom – you might find it easier to pop the strands in your mouth to hold them still and pull the ribbon out in front of you as you plait. Stop 5cm from the end of the ribbons, and tie another firm knot to keep the plaits from unravelling. Tie your new bracelet around your wrist, or the wrist of your best friend.

Bargain bangles

Don't bin old, shabby bangles; instead give them a material makeover. Any fetching fabric will do – a scarf, a piece of dress fabric, even a bit of leftover curtain material. Cut the fabric into strips and simply wrap them around the bangle, gluing as you go. Let it dry, and then pop it on your wrist.

How to make a button bracelet

The beauty of this bracelet is that you can make it in exactly the colours you want, so it can match any outfit. Or you can just have fun and cram on every colour under the sun.

You will need:

a handful of colourful shank buttons (these are the ones with the loop at the back)

elastic cord

Thread the buttons on to the elastic in any order you like – mix and match colours, old with new, plastic with metal. When you've got as many as you want, wrap it around your wrist as a measurement guide. Snip the elastic a little longer than you need and tie the bracelet to secure it with a simple knot.

> It's worth starting a button jar. Lovely buttons can be had for pennies at car boot sales and charity shops. And you can snip them off old cardigans, shirts and blouses.

Cuffs from old dresses

Look out for old dresses with beaded cuffs. The dress might not suit, but the cuffs can be made into brilliant bracelets, with minimum effort. All you have to do is carefully cut the cuffs away from the dress with a sharp pair of scissors (blunt blades will give an untidy raggedy edge). Use the cuff's buttons to fasten the beaded bracelets to your wrist.

A statement ring

Big buttons make bold statements. Head to your button box and select one big colourful button and one equally dramatic smaller button. Next you need a ring back, which you can buy in a craft shop, or use one from an old broken ring. Glue the little button on to the big button with good-quality craft glue. Then glue the ring back to the back of the big button. Let it dry completely.

Cheap chic watch

Transform an old watch using a dashing ribbon. Simply replace the old strap and fasten to your wrist with a timely bow.

A blooming brooch

An old brooch back, a fake flower and a pretend pearl can be transformed into a beautiful, bargain bloom. Pull the fake flower apart, discarding all the plastic bits. Squash it, so it's really flat and then glue it back together again. Once the reconstructed flower is dry, stick it on to the brooch back (if you haven't salvaged one from an old brooch you can buy new ones from craft shops). Glue the pretend pearl to the centre of the flower. And it doesn't have to be pearl: a rhinestone or a bijou button will be just as cute.

BARGAIN BEAUTY

In these cash-strapped times, spendthrift visits to the salon can be hair-raisingly expensive, but it's still possible to beautify on a budget. Cutting back doesn't mean doing without, so become a dab hand at mixing up store-cupboard staples for your money-saving makeover. It's all about looking good for less.

There are, however, a few things to take into account before embarking on a new routine:

- Always carry out a patch test.

- Avoid using on sensitive or damaged skin.

- Don't use if you're allergic to any of the ingredients.

- If any signs of irritation occur stop further use.

Heavenly hair

Salon hair needn't cost salon prices. Here are our superscrimpers top tips to put bounce in your bonce.

Trim the cost of a haircut

Give your bills the chop by volunteering as a hair model. Try searching for a free haircut on Gumtree or use Facebook to befriend your local salons and keep updated on the latest offers. And it's not just your hair: nails, eyelashes and make-up can cost a fortune, but not if you head to the trainees at beauty college.

Make shampoo go further

Pour a litre of water into a pan and bring to the boil. Add a couple of handfuls of fresh mint leaves, which have natural cleansing properties, and simmer for 20 minutes. Cool and strain. Funnel the minty liquid into half-empty bottles of shampoo to keep them going twice as long.

Canny conditioner

Deep-conditioning treatments can cost a tidy sum, but you can get a salon shine with the ordinary conditioner on your bathroom shelf.

Wash and towel-dry your hair as normal. Slather on conditioner generously, then put a carrier bag over your hair and wrap a warmed towel on top of it. Sit back and relax for 20 minutes or so. The heat from the towel will help your hair to absorb the conditioner. Rinse well and you'll have very lovely locks.

You can make your own conditioner by adding a tablespoon of honey to 500ml warm water and using it as the final rinse in your hair-washing regime. It will add a beautiful shine to your tresses.

Static hair

Fight flyaway hair with this simple tip: wrap your hairbrush in a silk scarf and use it to smooth down your hair, just as if you were brushing it. The silk neutralizes the static.

Lemon hairspray

The cellulose in the lemon will stiffen your hair in the same way as shop-bought hairspray. Cut a lemon in half and place in a saucepan with two cups of water. Bring to the boil, and bubble away until the liquid has reduced by half. Leave to cool. Pop a funnel in a spray bottle and pour in the lemony liquid. Store in the fridge and use within two weeks.

Fresh faced

If you're happy to put something inside your body, why not trust it to look after the outside, too? Try these kitchen ingredients to give yourself a first-class visage.

Parsley for problem skin

Parsley is a great circulation booster and good for flushing impurities from the skin. Chop finely and blend into a paste. Spread on to your face and leave for a few minutes. Rinse well.

Homemade hot-cloth cleanser

For clear, soft skin, pat a little olive oil into your skin – you don't need loads. Dip your flannel into warm water. Wring it out, and then lay the flannel over your face. Lie back for 15 minutes, rinse.

Bee spotless

Honey is a natural antiseptic and great for banishing spots. With a clean finger dab a little honey on to the affected area, cover with a plaster and leave overnight. You need to use untreated honey - honey that hasn't been heated before being sold - for this because heating destroys the honey's antibacterial and anti-inflammatroy properties.

Teeth whitener

Mix a teaspoon of bicarbonate of soda with a pinch of salt and brush your mouth with it. Rinse well with water afterwards.

Make foundation go further

Buy foundation one shade darker than your normal colour, blend it with cheap moisturizer and you have a tinted moisturizer.

Miracle Masks

Try these miracle masks to get you looking tip-top

Beautifying banana

Over-ripe bananas work brilliantly as a moisturizing facemask. Mash the bananas with a fork and apply them to your face with clean fingers. Leave for 10 minutes and rinse off with warm water.

For a face mask that's rich in vitamins B6 and C, potassium and manganese, beat a couple of egg whites with your mashed banana.

Marvellous mayonnaise

Yep, mayonnaise. Blob it on to your face, gently rub it in, leave for 5 minutes, and wipe clean with a tissue.

Youthful yoghurt

This homemade treatment straight from the fridge will have you looking as good as new.

You will need:
2 soluble aspirin
1 tsp water
2 tsp honey
1 tsp glycerine (available from most chemists)
35g natural yoghurt

Dissolve the aspirin in the water in a small bowl. Add the honey and then melt in the microwave until it's liquid. Stir in the glycerine, then top up with the yoghurt. Apply evenly to your face, and leave on for 15–20 minutes, then rinse off with fresh, warm water.

Grease-busting lemon

Lemon is brilliant at cutting through grease and impurities, and sugar is great for softening skin. Dampen a ball of cotton in the lemon juice, and then dap it in the sugar. Gently rub over your face in a circular motion. Rinse off with warm water.

Exfoliating oat

For glowing skin it's really important to exfoliate away the dead skin cells. An oat mask is just the thing to ditch dullness. Mix oats (any kind) with a tiny amount of water so that it forms a thick paste. Apply the paste to your skin, and leave for a minute or so. Rinse away with warm water.

BRIGHT EYES

They say the eyes are the windows to the soul, so use these thrifty tips to make sure yours are bright and beautiful.

Talc and mascara

To make your lashes lush and thick without spending a fortune on designer mascara, you need some old-fashioned talc. Apply a coat of ordinary mascara. Then, using your fingertips, coat your eyelashes with talc, making sure you don't get any in your eyes. Apply a second coat of mascara, and flutter your flattering lashes.

Longer-lasting mascara

When your mascara starts to dry out, try putting a couple of drops of olive oil on the wand and replacing the brush back into the tube. Give it a good wiggle around, but don't pump it in and out too many times.

> When the mascara really has all gone, rinse the wand out thoroughly and use it as an eyebrow brush.

Eye make-up remover

Petroleum jelly applied with cotton wool is just the ticket for removing tricky mascara.

LUSCIOUS LIPS

Pucker up with these penny-pinching smackers.

Glamorous lip gloss

Glossy and moisturising, this lovely balm also uses those hard
to get to stubs of lipstick that lurk in the bottom of the tube.
A lip-smackingly good idea!

You will need:

2 tsp beeswax (which you can buy online)

2 tsp coconut oil (you can find this in the supermarket)

2 tsp petroleum jelly

an old, but not out of date, lipstick

1 tsp honey

optional: edible glitter

a small travel pot

Mix the beeswax and coconut oil in a small bowl. Melt in the
microwave for 30 seconds on high then set aside to cool.

In a separate bowl blend together the petroleum jelly with the old
lipstick. Pour in the melted oil. Add the honey and the edible glitter
(if using) and stir everything together. Pour into a travel pot and
pop in the freezer for 15 minutes until the lip gloss hardens.

Note: Not suitable for those with nut allergies.

Lovely lip balm

Flavour this balm with whatever oil you fancy. This minty version has a lovely tingle.

You will need:

4g beeswax (which you can buy online)
16ml almond oil
peppermint oil (or any flavour of your choice)

small containers – salvaged mint tins, or mini jam jars are perfect.

Put the beeswax and almond oil in a heatproof bowl. Place the bowl over a pan of hot water (make sure the bowl doesn't touch the water). Wait until the oil and wax have nearly melted and then add in the peppermint oil. Carefully pour your new balm into containers and leave to cool before applying with your fingers.

Hands

Your hands put up with a lot. Give them a treat with these thrifty remedies.

Getting more out of your hand cream

You may think your tube of hand cream is empty, but there's often product lurking in the corners. Cut the tube a third of the way down, scoop out the freshly discovered cream from the lid end, and put it in the end of the tube. Use the cut off top part of the tube as the new lid.

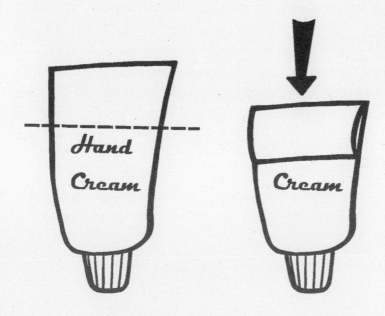

Natural oils hand cream

This entirely natural hand cream is rich and soothing. The wax helps protect your hands from the elements.

You will need:

30g beeswax (jars of honey sometimes come with the comb, or else it's available cheaply on the internet or from your local Asian supermarket)

60g cocoa butter

60ml palm oil

60ml oil (the lighter the better – ideally grape oil, but hemp oil or soya is fine)

10 drops of glycerine liquid (available from most chemists)

10 drops of aloe vera

1 tbsp ice-cold water

a sterilized jar

Put the beeswax, cocoa butter and palm oil in a small pan. Add the light vegetable oil. Warm through, until the oils have dissolved, and remove from the heat.

Add the glycerine and aloe vera – the glycerine attracts water to itself, which is how moisturizers work. Remove from the heat.

Whisk the mixture with an electric whisk. As you whisk, drip in a little cold water to the mix. As if by magic, it will turn into a rich hand cream.

While the cream is still warm spoon into a sterilized jar.

HANDY SCRUBS

Smooth hands will soon be yours. Scrub away the years with one of these kitchen store-cupboard potions.

Lovely lemon

Spoon granulated sugar into half a squeezed-out lemon skin and rub it over your hands. The sugar acts as an exfoliant and the lemon is a natural cleanser. Rinse off with warm water, and moisturize by rubbing a tiny drop of olive oil into your skin.

Salt and lemon olive oil

Pour a little olive oil into a small bowl and warm it very slightly in the microwave or over a pan of hot water (to help it absorb more easily into the skin). Mix in some sea salt, which acts as an exfoliant. Squeeze over some lemon juice – or the juice of any other citrus fruit – and mix together. Apply to your hands and rub the mixture into your skin for a couple of minutes, then rinse with warm water. Your hands will be beautifully moisturized and exfoliated.

Almond and honey

Store-cupboards essentials are great for making beauty products. For an exfoliating hand scrub mix together olive oil with ground almonds and honey and massage into your hands. Rinse with warm water.

Luxury hand treatment

Add a few drops of vanilla extract to 2ml of olive oil and massage into your hands for silky smooth skin.

Store-cupboard salve

The eggs and oats in this salve will quench even the driest of hands, restoring them to their former supple glory.

You will need:

egg

oats

ground almonds

sweet almond oil

a drop of jasmine oil (or any other essential oil that you like the smell of)

Mix everything together in a small bowl and smooth into the skin. This salve needs to be used quickly as the eggs won't stay fresh for long. It can be stored in a clean jar n the fridge.

Gleaming nails

If your nails are looking discoloured, squeeze the juice of a lemon into a bowl and then dip your fingers in the juice for a few minutes – the longer you leave them the whiter your nails will be.

How to revive old nail polish

Pop a couple of drops of nail-polish remover into the bottle of clogged-up nail varnish. Shake and it will be as good as new.

Skip-the-salon manicures

It's easy to achieve salon-stylish nails at home. Here are some ideas.

Fashionably French

Those sticky paper reinforcements you use for punched holes are the secret solution to perfectly semi-circular-tipped nails. Paint a base coat over your nails and let it dry. Cut the reinforcements in half and place them a little way down from the top edge of your nail. Apply a contrasting colour to the top of the nail along the semicircle sticker, and then whip off the sticker.

Glittery glamour

Spread out a sheet of old newspaper. Apply a base coat of clear nail polish. Let it dry to tackiness and then dip your nails in little pots of glitter. Use a cotton bud to dust off the excess glitter from your fingers. Fix in place with a clear top coat.

Wildcat

Go wild with leopard print nails. Paint on a base coat, the brighter the better. Let it dry. Choose a contrasting colour and dab on some spots over the base coat. Once the spots are dry, take a liquid eyeliner and outline the edges of the spots. You can free-style with some little lines and dots, too. Leave to dry completely and then protect with a clear top coat.

Polka party

For perfect polka dot nails you don't need to go dotty with your dosh. All you need is a kirby grip and two contrasting nail polishes. Apply a base coat and let it dry. Dab a blob of the second colour on to a piece of paper. Bend the kirby grip back and dip the end into the polish. Carefully dot all over your nails.

Sassy stripes

The secret weapon to getting perfect stripes with your nail polish is sticky tape. Paint on a base coat and let it dry. Cut the sticky tape into thin little strips. Stick them on your nail, anyway you like – horizontally, vertically, diagonally, criss-crossed. Paint on a contrasting colour. Don't bother waiting for it to dry, whip off the sticky tape strips straightaway.

Body beautiful

Experience spa-style luxury on a supermarket budget.

Scrimping scrub

Mix granulated sugar with a tablespoon of olive oil, splash in a few drops of essential oil and store in a clean jar until you need to get scrubbing.

Scented super spray

Head for a well ventilated area. Pour rubbing alcohol (you can buy this online) into a spray bottle, top up with tap water and add a few drops of your favourite essential oil. Put the lid on, shake well and then spray. Lovely.

Supermarket own-brand sunscreen is just as effective as the more expensive products. Buy bigger sizes and decant into a handy handbag-sized container.

Coffee cellulite treatment

If you look at the ingredients in expensive cellulite cream, caffeine is often listed. Don't throw away your coffee grounds; instead, mix them into a paste with a little water and apply it to your wobbly bits.

LEGS AND FEET

The superscrimping way to perfect pins and twinkling toes.

Shaving foam fabulous

Your own hair conditioner is a perfect substitute for shaving foam for your legs. Smooth the conditioner on to your legs and shave as normal. The razor will glide easily and your legs will get a moisturizing treat at the same time.

Super-soft feet

There are loads of easy ways to give your feet a treat.

- All you need for soft, moisturized feet are a pair of cotton socks and a jar of petroleum jelly. Massage the jelly really well into your feet before you go to bed. Pop your socks on, hop under the covers and when you wake up in the morning your feet will be velvety.

- Mix granulated sugar with a couple of drops of peppermint oil and massage into your feet for a refreshing scrub.

- Pour some brown sugar into a bowl, add a little honey and mix to form a thick paste. Massage it into your skin – it's also very good on rough knees and elbows.

PERFUME

Look after your scents and the pounds will look after themselves.

Cool ways to store your perfume

The bathroom windowsill is the worst place to display bottles of perfume, aftershaves and nail varnishes if you want them to last. It may sound a tad eccentric but the fridge is the best place to store them. It keeps them cool, and protects them from the damaging effects of sunlight. If there's not enough room in the fridge, at least keep all your products in their packaging and away from the light.

Longer-lasting scent

The key to smelling gorgeous for longer is to layer your scent. Scented body lotion can be very expensive but you can achieve the same effect with cheap unscented moisturizer and your own perfume. Blob a little of the moisturizer on to your hand, and spray perfume on to the cream. Mix and then rub into your skin. This solution can't be stored, so only make it when you're going to use it.

Personalized perfume

Perfume comes with a hefty price tag, but with essential oils you can make your own fragrance for a fraction of the cost.

You will need:

a selection of essential oils (jasmine, ylang ylang, sandalwood and

juniper are popular, but the choice is yours)
1 tbsp vodka
2 tbsp de-ionized water (you can buy this from garages)

a pre-loved empty perfume bottle

Mix the vodka with 4 or 5 drops of each of the oils. (The vodka will help carry the scented oils.)

Add the de-ionized water – it contains fewer impurities than tap water – to prevent the scent from being overpowering. Decant your fragrance into the pre-loved bottle; a kitchen funnel will help do that task.

If you're giving the present as a gift, you can personalize the packaging, too. Pop the scent bottle in a recycled box, decorate with a sweet snapshot, and tie it all together with some lovely leftover ribbon.

Please note, that some essential oils should not be worn when pregnant.

BATH

Ahhhhh, and relax . . .

Bath bombs

Add fizz and fragrance to your bath with these brilliant bath bombs. Witch hazel is a natural astringent and anti-oxidant which helps tone and replenish your skin. You can buy specialized moulds, but ice-cube trays are easier to get hold of and they're much cheaper.

You will need:
4 tbsp bicarbonate of soda
2 tbsp citric acid (you can buy this from the baking section in the supermarket)
a sprinkling of dried flowers
1 tbsp olive oil
10 drops essential oil
a dash of food colouring
a spritz of witch hazel

a spray bottle

In a glass bowl mix together the bicarbonate of soda and citric acid. Add the olive oil, dried flowers, essential oil and food colouring and mix it all together. Spray in the witch hazel. Mould the crumbly mixture in your hand and then press it firmly into moulds or silicone ice-cube trays. Put them in the airing cupboard overnight and they're ready for bathtime.

Bath oil

Pour baby oil into a small bottle and add a little perfume. Screw the lid on tightly and shake the bottle, so that the concoction emulsifies. Have a little sniff; add a little more perfume, if needed. Then add to your bath water.

MONEY-SAVING
MAINTENANCE

'**PROPERTY EXPERTS RECOMMEND HOUSEHOLDERS SPEND 1% OF THE VALUE OF THEIR HOME ON IMPROVEMENTS PER ANNUM IN ORDER TO MAINTAIN ITS MARKET VALUE.**'

Source: www.thisismoney.co.uk

Home improvements can add up to serious money investments. But in these days of frugal finance it's time to change our wasteful ways by indulging in a spot of DIY.

Recycle and reuse is the order of the day. Spruce up your place, without lightening your wallet. Even small changes can have a big impact.

Tricks of the trade

Wallpaper

When choosing wallpaper keep in mind that you'll need extra paper to match up a big, bold pattern. And why not try a feature wall, rather than papering the whole room.

Wallpaper stripper

A cup of white vinegar in warm water will do the job of expensive solvents and machines. Make sure the water is warm, sponge the vinegar mixture on to the wall very generously, so that the wallpaper is really damp – the vinegar will help break down the adhesive and the paper will then be easy to scrape away with a scraper.

Wood stain

For a pale wood stain pop a handful of metal screws into a glass jar and cover white vinegar. Replace the lid and leave for a week. Remove the screws and you can use the liquid to stain the wood. For a darker, greyer look, add a teabag. But don't use this on antique wood.

Squeaky floorboards

Eeek, eeek, a squeaky floorboard can be a very annoying give away when you're quietly trying to sneak a snack from the fridge. Restore

silence by drilling a hole in the noisy floorboard through to the joist. Then screw in a screw; this should stop the board from rubbing on the joist. Before you start, be totally sure that there are no electrical cables or pipes under the board.

Replacing lino tiles around the toilet

Because tricky shapes are involved you might be reluctant to replace the floor covering around the loo, but it's fairly easy to do. Wear rubber gloves and carefully remove the old covering to use as a template. Unroll your new floor covering, face down and put the old one on top. Draw around the old covering, and then cut along the guides. The new covering should fit perfectly.

Replacing silicone sealer

It's essential that the sealer around your bath and sink is doing its job properly; leakage will cause damp, and that's a major problem. Better to fix it before it gets out of hand.

You will need:
methylated spirits
silicone

a sharp knife

To replace the silicone, first you need to scrape away the old stuff using a sharp knife. Be careful not to cut yourself. Then use methylated spirits and a clean cloth to wipe away any residue.

If you're resealing a plastic bath fill it half full with warm water before applying the new silicone. Plastic expands in the heat, so you need to know you're putting the sealant in the right place.

Cut the nozzle of the silicone tube at a right angle. This will make the silicone easier to apply and give a neater finish. When you've sealed all the way round the bath or the sink, dab your finger in a little water and run it along the silicone for additional smoothness, and to compress it in the corners.

This is really important: leave the silicone to dry for at least 8 hours. Don't have a bath or a shower and don't fill the sink. The silicone must dry properly to work effectively.

A vegetable solution to a broken light fitting

If you've ever tried to replace an old light bulb and the glass has come away in your hand with the metal bit still in the socket, then you need a carrot; and not just because they help you see in the dark. Turn the electricity off at the mains. Press the broad end of the carrot into the fitting and twist gently. The left-behind metal fittings will come away in the carrot. No carrot? Use a potato instead.

Treat a rusty saw

Don't buy new when old will do. A rusty saw can be revived with a piece of old candle. Rub the candle into the rust and teeth of the saw (but don't cut your fingers) and it will lubricate the metal.

Chewed-up screws

One of the frustrations of DIY is a screw that won't undo. But if you place a wide elastic band over the top of the screw head, use a bigger screwdriver, and apply a little pressure, the gnarly screw should twist itself free.

Perfect painting

A lick of paint is the easiest way to transform your living space. Here are some clever ways to cut down on extra costs.

Tidy trays

Cleaning out paint trays can be a hassle. But there's a stress-free solution: cover the tray with foil before you pour the paint in. When you've finished, peel back the foil, throw in the bin, and the tray is as clean as though it had never been used. You could also use a plastic bag tied around the tray.

Spruce up damaged paintbrushes

Don't give old brushes the brush off; they can easily be revived. Pop some household vinegar in the microwave for about 10 seconds. Put the brush in the vinegar and comb through the bristles with a fork. Put an elastic band around the bristles to keep them in place. As soon as it's dry, the brush will be as good as new.

A cheap cutting-in brush

You don't need to buy a second, smaller brush when you're at the cutting-in stage of painting; adapt your first brush with an elastic band. Wrap the band around the bristles at the base of the brush and then head for those tricky edges.

Perking up old paint

Often when you open old tins of paint you'll find a thick skin is covering the surface and gunk lurking beneath. Cut the leg off a pair of tights. Roll the leg over the top of a second, empty tin, and tip the old lumpy paint into the tights. The tights will act as a sieve, retaining all the nasty bits, and letting the clean paint flow through.

How to stop leftover paint from drying out

Put the lid on firmly then turn the tin upside down and let the paint run around the lid. The paint will form a seal, and keep the contents of the tin fresh.

Avoid paint running down the sides of the tin

Tie a piece of string tightly across the top of the open paint tin, from rivet to rivet. Dip your brush into the paint and then wipe the brush on the taut string; the excess paint will drip back into the can. Tea-break? Rest the brush across the string, and the handle remains gloriously paint free.

How to remove gloss paint from your hands

There's no need to spend lots of money on heavy-duty hand cleaners. Before you go to work with the gloss, coat your hands in petroleum jelly. It'll form a protective barrier between your skin and the paint. Wipe off the jelly and the paint will come off with it.

Cover ceiling water stains

If you paint emulsion over a water stain, the stain will bleed through. But there's no need to buy expensive sealer, just use ordinary gloss. It's oil based, so the stain won't come through, and it'll act as a seal, too. Then you can paint the emulsion straight over the top.

Re-use turpentine and white spirit

Don't chuck away the turpentine or white spirit that you've used to clean paintbrushes. Pour it into a jar with a screw-top lid. Screw the lid on and leave it in a really safe place, out of the reach of children, for a few weeks. Eventually the turpentine will separate from the paint. Pour the separated turpentine into another jar and then you can reuse it time and time again.

A cheap substitute for masking tape on windows

Cut some strips from an old newspaper, give them a quick dip in some water and pat them along the edges of the window. Masking tape often leaves glue on the glass when you peel it off, and you can't slide it in to place; newspaper strips solve both of these problems.

Get economical with your energy

No one likes to waste their energy – save it for better things.

Avoiding burst pipes

If you're gong away for a while and you want to avoid the hassle of burst pipes there's an easy and cheap solution. Turn your heating to 'constant'. Next turn the radiator valves up throughout the whole house. Then turn the thermostat to 10°C or to the frost sign, if you have one. This will keep your house just above freezing, and will keep the pipes from freezing, too, and it'll expend hardly any energy, so your heating bills will be low.

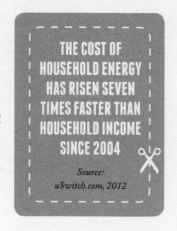

THE COST OF HOUSEHOLD ENERGY HAS RISEN SEVEN TIMES FASTER THAN HOUSEHOLD INCOME SINCE 2004

Source: uSwitch.com, 2012

Outside taps are very vulnerable in cold weather. To stop them freezing, turn off the water pipe to the outside tap. The isolation valve is usually located inside the house, but very close to the outside tap. Drain the water, by running the outside tap into a bucket. Leave the tap open. If there's any water left, it will have room to expand without bursting the pipes.

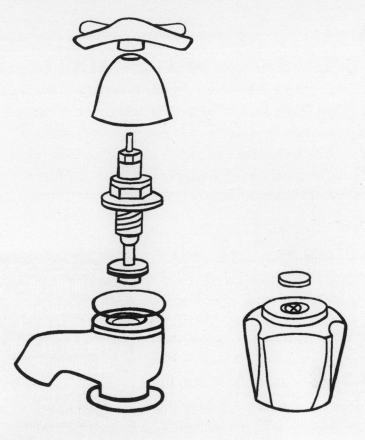

A drip, drip, dripping tap

Often it's a worn washer that's causing the problem. To replace it, turn off the water to the tap. Take the tap handle off and remove the valve body with an adjustable spanner. Wrap a small bit of toilet paper round the spout to stop it from being damaged. Undo the insert, and on the bottom you'll see the worn-out washer. Undo the small nut and ease the old washer up and out, and then pop the new one on, flat-side down. Put the nut back on and reassemble the tap in reverse order. Turn the water supply back on.

Detecting a leak in the loo

Dry the outside of the cistern and the toilet with a cloth. Take the lid off the cistern and add food colouring to the tank – choose a very vibrant colour. Leave it for about an hour. If there's coloured water in the toilet bowl then it's bad news and time to call in a professional plumber. But if you find a leak in the overflow pipe, you can mend it yourself by tightening the pipe as far as it will go.

Aerated showerheads

Aerated showerheads use less water that conventional ones, so you can cut down on your water bill. Head to the hardware shop and buy a new aerated showerhead. Unscrew your showerhead and check that the washer is there, then attach the new showerhead.

Bleeding radiators

Arm yourself with the radiator key and an old rag. Use the key to release the pressure valve (you'll usually find this at the top of the

radiator). Hold the rag under the valve to mop up any spillage. Once the water begins to trickle through, close the valve with the key. The trapped air should be out of the system.

A stuck radiator valve

If your radiators aren't getting warm, and you're sure that there's no air trapped in them, it could be that the valve is stuck shut. Remove the valve head, and you'll see a small pin. Grip a pair of grips around the pin and give it a little wiggle to get it free again. Pop on the valve head again. You should have a red-hot radiator, but without a scorching plumber's bill.

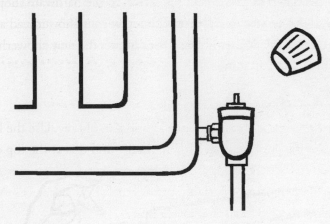

Clean radiators

Dust stops radiators from working efficiently, so a good clean can save you money. Wipe down with a cloth, and for those hard to reach areas, reach for a wire clothes hanger. Wrap a cloth around the hook, bend the body of the hanger and work your way in-between the radiator panels

A tip for tin foil

Make sure the radiator is turned off and cold to the touch. Cut a sheet of foil to the size of the radiator, or slightly bigger and put it behind the radiator, shiny side facing out. Wedge it in place with blu tack. The foil reflects the heat back into the room, so that's more heat, for less money.

Curtains from bed sheets

Old sheets can be given a new lease of life as curtains. Hem the top and the bottom of the sheets. Pin curtain-header tape to the top of the sheets and machine-stitch in place. And ring the changes colour wise, too: buy machine dye, read the manufacture's instructions and go to work. Wear rubber gloves to protect your hands, and old clothes. And buy some salt – most dyes need salt to stop the colour running.

Double the curtains, double the warmth

When the winter winds are blowing, cut down on draughts by hanging two pairs of curtains, one on top of the other, on every window to keep in all that lovely heat.

> Self-adhesive draught excluder strips stuck around windows and doors will help stop all that precious heat escaping in the wintry weather.

Newspaper

Not just useful for wrapping up today's fish and chips.

- Screwed-up old newspapers can be used as handy firelighters.

- Add a drop of vinegar to old newspaper and it is brilliant for cutting through dust and grime.

- Space in the freezer? Scrunch up some old newspaper and pop it into the gaps. This stops the freezer cooling empty spaces, so it works more efficiently.

- Add strips of newspaper to the compost heap to break down with your food scraps. Good compost should be 2-parts brown (paper, or cardboard, but not glossy types) to 1-part organic matter.

GLORIOUS GARDENING

24% OF US ARE NOW GROWING OUR OWN VEG. THAT'S MORE THAN EVER BEFORE!

Source: Which? 2011

Prune back on your expenditure, cut down on those pricy gardening products and make savvy savings in the garden with these down-to-earth tips.

BLOOMING MARVELOUS

Watering plants

Keep outdoor plants well watered by soaking newspapers in warm water and lining the plant trenches before putting in the plants.

A self-watering container for indoors

Self-watering containers can be very expensive, but you can easily make one with a plastic bottle and some string. The string uses capillary action to carry the water from the bottom of the container to the top, so that the plant waters itself.

You will need:
2-litre plastic bottle
65cm cord or string, made of natural fibre
pearlite or gravel
compost

black paint
sharp craft knife

Paint the top half of the bottle with black paint. This is to stop the light getting through to the compost (light can help promote algae growth, which is not the way forward for a healthy plant). Cut the bottle in half with a sharp knife and remove the lid.

Pour roughly 2cm of pearlite or gravel into the bottom of the clear half of the bottle. Double over the cord and drop it through the lid in the top half, holding on to it so that it doesn't fall through. Push the black half, lid-end down, inside the bottom half, leaving a few inches of space.

Scatter a little more pearlite or gravel into the top of the bottle and fill it with compost. Plant into the black half, water and then let science take over.

Keeping outdoor pot plants warm

The roots of plants need to be protected from the cold and frost. Before planting up, line the sides of your pot with bubble wrap. A little on the bottom is good, too, but don't cover up the drainage holes. Fill the bottom of the pot with compost, and tease out the roots of the plant to help it establish. Pop in the pot and then fill up with compost. For extra warmth drape plants in old net curtains in the cold winter months.

A clothes-hanger hook

Cheap metal clothes hangers can be made into hooks for hanging baskets. Cut off the sides of the hanger and make the hanger hook smaller using a pair of pliers. Curl the snipped ends into another hook. File down the sharp edges.

Storage tights

Use a clean pair of black tights to store spuds, onions or flower bulbs. Pop them into the leg of the tights and add some cloves of garlic. Black will prevent sun damage and the garlic will deter insects, who aren't big garlic fans. Hang the tights up to keep the vegetables out of the reach of mice and rats.

Frugal fertilizer

Plant feed can be expensive – and full of nasty chemicals. Try these natural fertilizers that won't cost you a penny.

- Add a bit of water to left over milk, and use the concoction as an indoor plant fertilizer, the calcium in the milk is good for growth.

- Clearing up after a party? Don't ditch the beer dregs. Pour them into a watering can, top up with water and use as a lawn fertilizer.

- Vegetable peelings, tea bags, grass cuttings, newspaper and cardboard boxes can all be made into compost (no plastics, animal products or non-biodegradable stuff). Drop them into a bin and cover with a mat. After a few weeks, you'll have compost.

Recipes by the Ministry of Food.
Gardening Instructions by the Ministry of Agriculture.

GROWING YOUR OWN

It can get pricey buying new plants for your garden year after year. Save a packet by growing your own from what's already growing in your garden. Share seeds with friends to mix up your marigolds and add some variety to your violets.

Leftover labelling

- Discarded margarine tubs are just the thing for making plant labels. Using scissors cut the sides of the tub into strips. Cut one end of the strip into an arrow shape. Write the name of the plant in marker pen and pop it into the soil, arrow-side down. Once it has served its petunia purpose, you can wipe the lettering off with a scourer for future fuchsias.

- Use your discarded ice-cream sticks as plant markers. Write on the name of the flower or herb with felt pen, and press into the soil next to the plant.

Seedling pots

Discarded polystyrene cups make fine seedling pots. Make a couple of drainage holes in the bottom of the cup with a screwdriver, put in some compost, sow the seeds, top with another layer of compost, and you've got an ideal, warm growing environment.

Recycled seed trays

Don't buy seed trays or plastic plant pots, instead raid the recycling bin for free containers. You can use yoghurt pots, fruit pallets and margarine tubs. Soft cardboard egg boxes are particularly good; the cardboard retains moisture and when the seedlings are ready to be transplanted the whole plant can be moved to its new position without disturbing the roots.

Cut-price cloche

Old plastic bottles work well as plant protectors. Cut the bottom off the plastic bottle and place the top bit of the bottle over the young seedlings, leaving the lid slightly ajar for ventilation.

Complementary planting

Interplant your fruits and vegetables with ornamental flowers. Lots of flowers – marigolds, for instance – will attract hover flies, and these insects love to munch on whitefly and black fly. So you can cut right back on the pesticide, and have a garden that's a joy to behold.

Sprouting spuds

If your potatoes have started to sprout, don't throw them away. Carefully peel them, and use the potato as usual. Then plant the peelings and in five months' time you'll have a small crop of potatoes.

Root vegetables

Root vegetables don't like having their roots disturbed when they're planted out. But if you plant them in the discarded cardboard tubes from the insides of toilet rolls, you'll avoid this trauma. Place the cardboard rolls in your seed tray and fill each tube with compost. Seeds should be planted indoors in February or March. As soon as the plants are big enough, dig a hole in the ground and pop the tube in. The card will rot away and fertilize the soil, and the root vegetables will be sprightly. This method also works brilliantly with sweet peas.

Clever containers

Update your garden as often as you like with these ingenious planters that cost a fraction of what you'd pay at the garden centre.

Pipe plant pots

A length of plastic pipe can make interesting-looking plant pots. Look out for discarded pipes in skips. Chop the pipe into sections of different lengths. Place the tubes vertically in the ground at varying heights, so that they look something like a larger version of a desk tidy. Pop a piece wood on the top of the pipes, and then hammer the pipes into the ground. Discard the wood. Plant the pipes up, and in a couple of months you'll have a living sculpture that's unique in shape and a riot of colour.

Tin plant pots

Empty tin cans can be transformed into handy plant pots. Tomato tins are particularly good as they have a white plastic lining that keeps the metal from rusting. Wash the cans thoroughly then bash holes in the base with a screwdriver and a hammer, for drainage. Fill with compost and press in new tomato plants.

Clay pots

Paint clay pots with blackboard paint. Plant them up with herbs or flowers and chalk their names on the outside of the pot for a designer flourish.

(See page 108 for more ideas for blackboard paint.)

Stony plant pots

Lots of people have a half-bag of cement lurking in their garage, and with a little effort, it can be turned into unique stone plant pots. Wear some rubber gloves, as cement can be a skin irritant, and always follow the manufacturer's instructions.

You will need:
cement
sand
stone chippings
1 large plastic plant pot

1 small plastic plant pot

bucket
a bit of wood
drill

Mix three parts sand to one part cement in a bucket. Add enough water to bind the mixture and stir to combine. Then mix in some stone chippings. Put about 8cm of the mix into the bottom of the larger plastic plant pot. Place the smaller plastic plant pot inside the bigger one, and squash it into the centre of the cement mix. Fill up the edges with the mix, and tamp it down with a bit of wood. Pat the sides of the big pot to compress the mix. Leave to set for 6–8 hours. Remove the outside pot, and then the smaller, inside one. If you like the polished look, simply drill drainage holes in the bottom and plant up your new container. For a rougher finish, rub the outside with a trowel, and then drill the drainage holes.

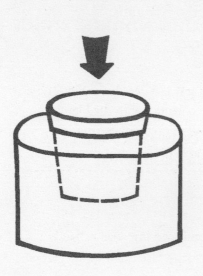

Sink salad

Old sinks can become perfect miniature vegetable gardens. Put some old crocks in the base for drainage, fill it with compost, and plant some lovely lettuces and ravishing radishes.

An eccentric garden planter

A seatless chair and an old enamel bowl are a perfect partnership. Plant up the enamel bowl with flowers of your choosing, then rest it where a bottom should go.

A colander hanging basket

An old colander and a blanket or jumper can be transformed into a blooming hanging basket. Line the colander with the blanket or jumper. Fill it with compost, and plant up. Strawberries and tumbling, trailing lobelias look especially nice.

Homemade elastic bands

Past-their-best rubber gloves can be snipped into elastic bands. Lay the gloves flat and cut into thin strips. Use them in the garden as plant ties.

Sprucing up garden furniture

White plastic garden furniture can get very grubby if it's left outside, but don't worry, you can bring it back to life. Wearing rubber gloves, dissolve two dishwasher tablets in a bucket of warm water – the dishwater tabs contain a bleaching agent. Scrub the furniture well, and then leave some of the liquid on the plastic. Rinse off 15 minutes later. Buff with an old towel and you'll have furniture fit for summer.

Vertical planting

Decide where you want your planter to reside and construct it there, as the finished project is very heavy and will be difficult to cart around. Swaying grasses work well planted along the top of the pallets, while hanging plants such as ivies and tumbling tomatoes are perfect for the sides.

You will need:

3 pallets
tarpaulin or
weed-suppressing fabric
4–5 bags of compost
staple gun
drill and screws
knife or sharp scissors

Knock out the middle staves at the back of two of the pallets and cover each one with tarpaulin, leaving a little excess at the sides, stapling it in place. Stand the pallets so that they are vertical and, with the fabric on the inside, screw both pallets together across the top and along the bottom. Overlap the excess fabric at the sides and staple it neatly to the sides of the pallet. You should now have a giant container with a gap in the top.

To keep your planter stable, screw a third pallet to one side at a 90-degree angle. Now you can fill the space inside the vertical pallets with soil and plant up to your heart's desire. Plant into the gap at the top and make slits in the tarpaulin at the sides and press plants into the hole.

Wonderful wildlife and pesky pests

Attract the right guests and evict those annoying gatecrashers with these thrifty tips.

Cheap cheeps

Make these pretty birdseed cakes and you'll have feathered friends flocking.

You will need:
cereal
chopped fruit from the fruit bowl
birdseed
sunflower hearts
gelatine
100ml boiling water

2L plastic bottle
craft knife
stapler
twine
tin foil

Chop of the top of the bottle, and then chop off the bottom, too. Cut the middle of the bottle into 3cm-strips – these are going to be the moulds for the birdseed cakes. Staple the strips into a teardrop shape, make two holes at the top and thread the twine through.

Mix the cereal, fruit, birdseed and sunflower hearts together in a bowl. In a separate bowl mix the gelatine with 100ml of boiling water and stir briskly. Add a small amount of the dissolved gelatine to the seed mix. It should be enough to coat them, but not to soak them.

Put the mould on to a sheet of foil and spoon the seed mixture into the mould. Compress the seeds with the back of a spoon. Put in the fridge overnight to set.

Hang from a tree or a trellis, and watch as goldfinches, bullfinches and green finches head over for dinner.

• •

A bird feeder

Watch as the birds balance on either side of this clever feeder. Use sticks from your garden for a natural look.

You will need:
2L plastic bottle
2 sticks
birdseed
twine

craft knife
drill
funnel

Thoroughly wash the plastic bottle. Cut a 1cm-slit in the middle of the bottle and make another alongside it, then join up the slits to make a small flap. Make another flap on the opposite side of the bottle. Make another two flaps towards the bottom of the bottle in the same way. Push the flaps up into the bottle; this will stop the seeds from running out. Make holes beneath each of the flaps, and push a stick through them to make two perches.

Unscrew the lid and drill a hole in it. Thread twine through the hole, knotting it under the cap. Funnel birdseed into the bottle and screw the lid back on. Hang up the feeder by the twine. And put out some water, too – the birds will be glad of a drink and a bath.

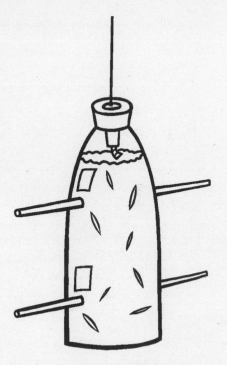

• •

Birdhouse boot

It may not be the most attractive of options, but an old boot makes a cosy bird home.

Clean and disinfect the boot first and add new daubing to make it waterproof. Loosely tie the laces. Use a big plastic plant pot for the roof, by cutting off the sides of the plant pot. If you want something a little more picturesque, use some painted cast-off pieces of wood – a discarded pallet would be fine. Screw the boot to the tree, and screw the pot or wooden roof above it.

CD scarecrows

Sunday supplements frequently give away free CDs. They're useful even if you never play them. Thread them on to string and attach the string to a garden cane. Position the cane in the garden and the shiny reflection from the CDs will frighten birds away from young plants.

Bird scarers

Place old plastic bottles on the end of garden canes. Not only do they keep the birds at bay, they also prevent a poking-in-the-eye accident.

Slug deterrent

Crush up some leftover eggshells, and use them to make a little fence around tender, young plants. Slugs cannot bear slithering on scratchy surfaces.

Slugs and snails

Slug pellets are expensive and bad for wildlife and pets, but bran is brilliant. Use any bran-based cereal and put it in the garden, overnight, under a large lettuce or cabbage leaf. The slugs and snails will be attracted to the smell of the bran, and will hide under the leaves. In the morning pick up the slug- and-snail-filled leaves, and then dispose of them as you see fit.

Pest control

You don't need to spend loads on specialist pesticides; instead put a few squirts of everyday washing-up liquid in a bucket of water (you could even use your old washing-up water) and then decant the mixture into an old spray bottle. Spray on plants affected by whitefly, greenfly and black fly. Make sure to douse the whole plant; the nibblers love to hide where the leaves join the stem, and especially around new growth. Use it frequently to ward off the pesky pests.

Weed control

Special weed-control fabric is sold in garden centres and comes with a hefty price tag. But you could use a bulky builder's bag for next to nothing. Look in skips for discarded ones, or head to your local builders' yard.

Cut the bag to fit your container, place it on top of the container and tuck the edges inside. Make a slit down the middle of the fabric and plant your plants through the slit. Cover the fabric in bark or mulch, and look forward to weed-free gardening.

Weed killer

To get rid of the weeds between paving stones, pour salt along the line of the weeds and then pour boiling water over the salt, making sure it goes down between the cracks. The weeds will be gone within a few days.

DRIVING A HARD BARGAIN

The average British car owner spends £713 on maintenance each year.

Source: www.rac.com

The cost of running a car can cause palpitations, but we all need to get from A to B. Don't be frightened of your engine. Keep your car's manual handy and you'll soon learn what's what.

These handy hits will keep your motor running for longer and save you expensive trips to the professionals.

Frugal fuel consumption

As fuel prices rise and rise, follow these superscrimping tips to help you use less.

Fuel savings

Drive in the highest gear possible. Gears four and five are the fuel-economy gears, so these are the ones you should be aiming for. Also, keep the interior and exterior of your car clean and free from clutter – remove roof bars, empty the boot, and chuck out the rubbish accumulated under the seats.

Fuel economy

Don't fill the tank to the brim, this adds weight to the car and a heavier vehicle uses more fuel. A half-full tank means more economical fuel use. In summer, don't use the air conditioning, it makes the engine work harder and you'll use more fuel. Too hot? Open the window.

Get Appy

Use the Highways Agency's App to get the latest news on traffic jams and road works to avoid a fuel-guzzling snarl up. Also check out Apps where you can type in the make, model and year of your car for tips on how to drive more economically.

Cleaning interiors

You don't need to buy a new car; just give your old one a spring clean. Scented hanging fir tree ornament, optional.

Brilliant baby wipes

Baby wipes are brilliant for restoring the shine to dull plastic in the car's interior. They'll get rid of all that ground-in grime and grease.

A sweet-smelling car

A build up of algae can cause bad pongs in the air conditioning. Algae treatments can cost hundreds of pounds, but with an essential oil (lavender is a popular choice) and some baby oil you can sort out the nasty niffs yourself. Mix the essential oil and the baby oil together and, with a dropper, squeeze about 10 drops of the scented mix into each of the air conditioning vents. Leave it for a couple hours so that the fragrance infuses and kills the bacteria. Next time you switch on the heating or air conditioning, the smell will have changed from hellish to heavenly.

Spotless car seats

Mix bicarbonate of soda with white vinegar and dab on to stains on the car seat with an old toothbrush. Leave for 20 minutes and then hoover it up. But don't use this on leather upholstery.

Car carpets

Sprinkle bicarbonate of soda on smelly car carpets and add a few drops of lavender oil. Leave for 30 minutes then come back and vacuum up the soda and the smells.

Cleaning exteriors

Save yourself a trip to the carwash and restore your car's enviable gleam.

Cleaning the windscreen

A dab of methylated spirits on a clean rag works wonders on windows. Clean with a circular motion, and then buff with a soft cloth. Clean the wiper blades in the same way, so you won't be smearing fresh dirt on to your sparkling screen. Also, try dabbing vinegar on to kitchen paper and wiping the blades. This will soften the rubber and the wipers will work much better

How to clean clogged wiper squirters

The small holes in the wiper squirters can get clogged up with muck. Open a safety pin, wiggle it the holes and all will become clear.

Brighten up dull paintwork

A re-spray can cost thousands, but you can spruce up the paintwork on your car for just a few pounds. Buy a good liquid car polish and a very gentle face-exfoliating cream. Mix two parts exfoliating cream to ten parts polish. Dab a cloth (old, clean T-shirts are perfect for this chore) in the mix and rub it over the car very thoroughly. Let it dry and then buff it with a clean cloth for a superior shine.

Dreaded droppings

Bird droppings are acidic, so don't be tempted to peel them away from your car; even if the dropping is dry it'll still leave behind a damaging mark. Drown the offending item in warm soapy water and when it's soft, wash it away. Remove the final residue with a mix of good-quality car polish and a few drops of baby oil. Rub in the oil and polish with a clean rag, leave it to dry completely and then buff with a soft, clean cloth.

....

Cleaning alloy wheels

Scuffed alloy wheels can make the rest of your car look shabby. To get them gleaming again use a mild scouring pad and some washing-up liquid, and gently rub into the alloys. Make sure there are plenty of bubbles and take it nice and slowly. When the scuffs have disappeared, rinse with cool water. Dry, and then give the wheels a good polish to protect them.

....

Revive black car trims

Black shoe polish and a shoe brush will do the job. Imagine the trims are boots and get polishing

Maintenance

You shouldn't attempt a complete engine overhaul unless you're an expert, but there are a few problems you can solve without calling out the rescue team.

Unsticking car windows

A household candle is the perfect lubricant for a sticky car window. Wind the window down and scrape the candle along the channels that the windows run in. Wind the window up again and this time it'll glide.

How to unstick a seized car lock

When the temperature drops, car locks can get temperamental. You don't need an expensive lubricant; the magic solution is a safety pin and some washing-up liquid. Open up the safety pin and put it in the lock. Squeeze some washing-up liquid into the lock, wiggle the pin back and forth so that the liquid spreads all around. Result? A working lock.

Change the air filter

The air filter stops dirt, mud, muck and leaves getting into the engine, but it often gets blocked, and the car uses more fuel as a consequence. If you change the air filter your car will be perkier, and there'll be less pollution being pumped out through the exhaust.

Check the car's make and model and get the right one for
your vehicle.

Checking the car battery

Take a 2p coin and twist off each of the cells in the car battery.
Have a quick peek at the electrolyte plates inside; they should be
covered in distilled water. If they're dry, the battery won't charge
properly. Top up each cell with distilled water, and put the cell
covers back on. Charge the battery in the normal way.

How to check for an exhaust leak

Make sure you are in a well-ventilated space. Keep the engine
running and clamp a damp rag over the end of the exhaust. Be
careful not to burn your hand. If there's a leak, you'll be able to see
the exhaust fumes spilling out somewhere – from the front, centre
or back of the exhaust. Forewarned is forearmed, and you'll be able
to tell the garage exactly where the problem is, and avoid shelling
out for a whole new exhaust pipe.

Engine coolant

Low levels of engine coolant (also known as antifreeze) can lead to
major engine damage. Check your handbook for the engine coolant
container.

Don't take the top off when the engine is hot – the temperature
can reach a scalding 95°C. Pour in antifreeze a little at a time.
The radiator should also have a little antifreeze, too, mixed in
with the water.

Check the oil

You should do this at least once a week. If the oil runs dry, it can add up to hundreds of pounds in repair bills. Use the dipstick to measure the oil level, and always make sure the engine is cold when you're doing this. If the engine is hot the oil expands and it will give you a false reading. Check where your oil goes in your car manual. Funnel in the oil in small drops, don't over fill, and re-check the level with the dipstick.

SEVENTY PER CENT OF CAR OWNERS NEVER CHECK THE OIL LEVELS IN THEIR VEHICLE.

Source: Swinton

An impromptu oil funnel

If your car desperately needs oil and you are funnel-less, roll a newspaper into a cone shape, unscrew the oil filter cap, put the newspaper funnel in and pour in as much oil as you need. This will stop excess oil spilling on to the engine or the exhaust, which is a fire risk. DO NOT use this method for fuel or brake fluid and always carefully dispose of the oil-soaked paper.

Fitting new windscreen wipers

You can fit new wipers in seconds. Underneath the wipers are tiny pips, like buttons. Press down on these to release the blades, and then remove them. Feed the new blade on and press into place.

Topping up windscreen wash

Driving without screen wash can result in an MOT fail, a mucky windscreen and a police fine.

Water on its own won't do the job, and too much screen wash will smear the window. Dilute the screen wash with water; about ten to fifteen per cent screen wash is ideal. Check your manual if you're unsure where the screen wash should go.

THIRTY-NINE PER CENT OF UK MOTORISTS DRIVE WITHOUT SCREEN WASH.

Source:
www.webuyanycar.com

Mix your own windscreen wash

Mix three cups of cheap household window cleaner into a gallon of water. To make it easier to pour it into the car's windscreen reservoir, tip the liquid into an old plastic bottle.

Tyre tread check

Worn tyre treads can cost you three points on your driving licence and a hefty fine, as well as being dangerous. To make sure they're safe to drive on, use the 20p check. Place the coin in the tyre treads and if you can see any of the 20p poking out, the tyre needs replacing.

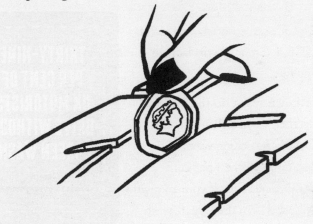

Ignition

Car ignitions can get worn out. An easy way to save wear and tear is to make sure that your car key ring has only one key on the ring. That way the ignition isn't loaded down with extra, unnecessary weight and it'll last longer as a result.

DIRECTORY

These handy websites might just help you save a mint.

Food and cooking

Use a supermarket comparison site to get the best prices and offers:

www.supermarket.co.uk
www.mysupermarket.co.uk
www.comparesupermarketprices.co.uk

For cheaper food, buy in bulk direct from suppliers. To check membership and fees, go to:

www.uk.coop
www.costco.co.uk
www.Booker.co.uk

For free, safe-to-eat foraged food look at:

www.foragersapp.com
www.eatweeds.co.uk

Clothes and fashion

Too many clothes? Try swishing. Photograph your unworn clothes, and upload the pictures to sites such as :

www.swishing.co.uk
www.Swishing.com
www.Swishingparties.com

For designer and good quality clothing you could try:

www.hardlyeverwornit.com
www.vestiairecollective.com
www.champagneandlemonade.com

For second-hand wedding dresses try:

www.sellmyweddingdress.co.uk
www.stillwhite.co.uk

If you're looking for inspiration for ways to re-fashion your own clothes check out www.traidremade.com - an online shop which gets fashion students to re-style clothes which would otherwise be binned.

Wesbites like:

www.webuyanyclothing.com
www.cashclothes.org.uk
www.clothesbank.co.uk

buy bulk lots of clothes and pay per kilo.

Beauty

To find a beauty school near you, check out:

www.beautyfinder.co.uk

Crafts

For cut price craft materials join:

www.scrapstoresuk.org

You can buy and sell crafty stuff on

www.Ebay.co.uk

www.Etsy.co.uk

• •

Money-making

Car booting has become a national pastime. If you have a stash
of stuff to sell, turn up early to get a good pitch. It's a good idea
to offer free carrier bags, as that encourages bulk buying. And don't
be afraid to discount goods at the end – getting 50p for something
is better than nothing. Things that sell well include toys, children's
clothes and bric-a-brac.

These websites will tell the times and venues of your local boot fares:

www.carbootjuncion.com

www.carbootsales.org

www.carboot.com

www.yourbooty.co.uk

A great new way to raise cash is to sell your old technology. On-line
stores will buy old mobile phones, laptops, tablets and cameras.

www.cashinyourgadgets.co.uk

www.weeebuy.co.uk

www.gadgets4everyone.co.uk

If you think you have some hidden treasures at home, take them
to a shop specialising in Antiques and Collectables:

www.Antiquedealerfinder.co.uk

To sell your gold jewellery try:

www.tescogoldexchange.com
www.Lois-jewellery.com

You can earn up to a certain amount of money by renting out a room in your house without having to pay tax on it. You can find a lodger for free on listing sites such as Student Notice Board and Gumtree. Specialist sites like SpareRoom, EasyRoommate and RoomBuddies may charge a small fee. Remember, always check references and ask about any criminal convictions.

www.studentnoticeboard.com
www.gumtree.com
www.spareroom.co.uk
www.easyroommate.com
www.roombuddies.com

You could set up your garden out as a mini camping site. Although the season is mainly limited to the summer, you can charge from around five pounds per person per night. You must provide access to a toilet and running water, but can choose to offer additional facilities like wifi or off-street parking.

www.campinmygarden.com

Or rent out your parking site:

www.yourparkingspace.co.uk
www.parkatmyplace.co.uk
www.parkatmyhouse.co.uk

Going out

It's always worth checking online voucher sites for special deals on local restaurants:

www.toptable.com
www.squaremeal.co.uk
www.vouchercloud.com
www.vouchercodes.co.uk/restaurant-vouchers.

78% of us have thrown away money-off vouchers… but in these tough times, we should make use of them:

www.vouchercloud.com
www.vouchercodes.co.uk
www.voucherseeker.co.uk

And there are student discount web sites that will give you money off almost anything you could think of

www.nus.org.uk
www.thestudentbeans.com

There are websites where you can exchange everyday services like housekeeping or pet walking:

www.letslinkuk.net
www.swapaskill.com

Holidays

For free or cheap days out:

www.netmums.com

www.dofreestuff.com

www.dayoutwiththekids.co.uk

www.kidsdaysout.co.uk

www.nationaltrust.org.co.uk

www.ramblers.org.uk

www.nationalparks.gov.uk

www.naturalengland.org.uk

www.farmgarden.org.uk

Cheap train travel

Book in advance through National Rail Enquiries' Cheapest Fare
Finder tool, or through your train operator's site. You can also
subscribe for email ticket alerts from thetrainline.

www.nationalrail.co.uk

www.thetrainline.com

To find out how you could benefit from the cycle-to-work scheme
visit the cycle to work alliance or cycle-to-work guarantee websites.

www.cycletoworkalliance.org.uk

www.cycletoworkguarantee.org.uk

For cheap holiday rooms try:

www.yha.org.uk

3.2 million savvy Brits have already caught on to the idea of swapping their homes with like-minded holiday makers. It's a straight swap so your accommodation costs nothing. To find people to swap with you can register on one of the many house swap websites. Expect to pay around twenty pounds for an annual subscription.

www.intervac.co.uk
www.homelink.org.uk
www.exchangeaway.com
www.u-exchange.com

Check your home insurance too – a swap partner is a non-paying guest and most insurers will acknowledge you're at lower risk from burglary because your home is occupied. However you could invalidate your policy by not telling them. So let them know.

Foreign currency exchanges are a minefield. The easiest way to guarantee that you get the most for your money is to use a comparison website:

www.travel-money.org
www.compareholidamoney.com
www.currencies.co.uk

INDEX

This book is published to accompany the television series entitled *Superscrimpers*, which is produced by Remarkable Television, part of Endemol UK Ltd, for Channel 4.

Executive Producers: Helen White and Oliver Wright
Series Producer: Claire Campbell
Creative Director: Colette Foster

Published in 2013 by Square Peg
10 9 8 7 6 5 4 3 2 1

Text by Eithne Farry
Copy edited by Laura Herring
Design and decorative illustrations by Lucy Stephens
Practical drawings by Ella Carroll

The Random House Group Limited Reg. No. 954009

Addresses for companies within The Random House Group Limited can be found at: www.randomhouse.co.uk

A CIP catalogue record for this book is available from the British Library

ISBN 978 0 22 409605 8

The Random House Group Limited supports the Forest Stewardship Council (FSC®), the leading international forest certification organisation. Our books carrying the FSC® label are printed on FSC®-certified paper. FSC® is the only forest certification scheme endorsed by the leading environmental organisations, including Greenpeace. Our paper procurement policy can be found at www.randomhouse.co.uk/environment

Mixed Sources
Product group from well-managed forests and other controlled sources
www.fsc.org Cert no. TT-COC-2139
© 1996 Forest Stewardship Council
FSC

Printed and bound by CPI Group (UK) Ltd, Croydon, CR0 4YY

To buy books by your favourite authors and register for offers, visit www.randomhouse.co.uk

Picture credits:
Photographs on pages 8, 83, 89, 102, 136, 149, 162, 186, 191, 204, 213, 228, 234 courtesy of Getty Images; pages 23, 25, 29, 64, 71, 74, 97, 145, 177, 203, 211, courtesy of Alamy; pages 126 and 194 courtesy of The Advertising Archives.

Thank You

A very special thank you to Mrs Moneypenny and our army of fabulously thrifty Superscrimpers.

Thanks also to Katie Boyd, David Sayer and Karoline Copping at Channel 4; Colette Foster, Catherine Welton, Anya Francis, Debb Swindells, Oliver Wright, Louise Banks, Natalie Flageul and Claire Heys at Endemol; Eithne Farry, Lucy Stephens, Ella Carroll and the team at Square Peg.

Thank You